Royal Borough
of Windsor &
Maidenhead

D1346489

THE **MODERN ITALIAN** COOK

JOE TRIVELLI

THE MODERN ITALIAN COOK

SEVEN DIALS

To Matilda and Antonietta

CONTENTS

INTRODUCTION

ON ARRIVAL AT BOLOGNA AIRPORT I crawled into the rear of the family car, finally back in Italy after a long day of delays. A few years into a cooking career in London I felt like a child once more and both home and away at the same time. The folks were en route from my aunt Dina's; I had missed her lunch and was famished, so they passed me a picnic box she had packed for me. I ate in the dark without being able to see what was inside – an artichoke stuffed with bread, cheese and olives. It remains one of the best things I have ever eaten. It tasted like it had been well cooked but it didn't fall apart and, to my delight, there were two – a complete meal. I felt simultaneously a tremendous pride in coming from a family who could cook so well, while appreciating the exoticism in comparison to my British heritage. I felt a sense of belonging and a sense of otherness. That is very much the standpoint of this book – a sort-of Italian cookbook written in London. About there and here, near and far.

Several times when I was growing up we were taken to an expat Italian picnic. It was near Bedford, I think. I don't know if it still happens. Organised by some cultural association, Italian families gathered, mostly around parked cars, and cooked pasta together. All the teenagers were incredibly well groomed, with American shades, making me feel like a boy from the provinces. I longed to be as cool. Everyone came Italian camping-style, bringing every last creature comfort, while Dad tried to improvise a table with whatever he found lying around. We didn't really know anybody there, but I felt that same sense of connection, of being at once the same but different.

I was born hungry. Family folklore has it that, aged two, I ate a whole egg with the shell on because my aunt couldn't peel it quickly enough. My nickname was 'Lasagne' for a time, when I demonstrated, at my fifteenth birthday, the prodigious amount of Mum's good food that I could eat. My brother, Giacomo, joked that I must have fallen into the sugo – sauce – as Obelix did in the magic potion. My approach in this book is my own, intricately linked with my Anglo-Italian heritage. It is a reflection of my mornings drinking a mug of tea while I make my espresso. It's about trips away and returning with ideas. Or ideas that just leap out of the fridge. About quick suppers and longings for tastes and ingredients remembered from far away. It is not an anthropological cultural study, rather a ragtag of ideas that I have cooked with ingredients more or less easily available.

Cooking Italian food has consumed me for the last twenty years, yet despite this I often feel like I am just at the start, so wonderful is its range and breadth. Cooks, writers and food historians who approach the subject face a Tantalean task, which has resulted in three main categories of Italian cookbook: the traditional (authentic and reverential); the simple (focusing on how quick and easy Italian cooking can be); and the regionally focused (from the Alps of Bolzano to Mount Etna in Sicily). I've bought them all, many twice over. As I relocated flat to flat to flat they saw many kitchens, lots of action, and I lost the fight to keep them clean.

In this book I offer a modern perspective on, and practical approach to, how we are cooking and eating Italian food today. This is a book that capitalises on the fact that the supermarket, as well as the specialist shop, has keyed into the popularity of Italian produce, giving us all easy access to better ingredients. I can't emphasise enough how different this is from when I first started to cook professionally in 1995. At the same time, it understands the limitations of living in cooler climes in terms of food that is locally grown, as well as the opportunity of having different produce largely unavailable in Italy.

I HAVE WORKED AT THE RIVER CAFÉ since 2001, five years after the restaurant's founders, Ruth Rogers and Rose Gray, published their first book, or the 'Blue Book' as it became known. Its success was instant and sparked a wave of Italian-themed dinner parties. Suddenly everyone was searching for cavolo nero for the famous *ribollita* (Tuscan bread soup), me included. When I first started, people were still ringing the kitchen asking for tips to fine-tune such-and-such a recipe. Rose and Ruthie had a special kind of magic that worked not only on everyone who came to the restaurant but on those who bought, and cooked from, their book. They shaped my career and eventually afforded me the opportunity to earn a living the only way I know how: as a chef. I'm massively proud to be part of the River Café family; I have felt, and still feel, sheltered and protected by them. Working there, I get to write fresh menus every day; interact with incredible produce; and bore my colleagues about what I might cook at home that evening. It's a privilege to be part of Ruthie's beautiful kitchen, flooded with light and the best ingredients. I have never taken it for granted.

I think the cliché of the chef who goes home to beans on toast is true. But in my case, it's 'what toast, with which beans?' Cooking for me has never been a hassle but a

pleasure, and what I hope to communicate most of all in this book is *il piacere di cucinare*: the joy of cooking. I have never stopped cooking at home, even when I was a very young cook earning my colours with six or seven shifts a week, some of them doubles. I remember reading a famous French chef who said that his last food on earth would be a grilled red mullet caught from a certain part of the Mediterranean. It's a clever answer, because it states the perfection of simplicity. Yet this same chef ran a restaurant that epitomised pretension in dining. I have always cooked at home as I cook at work: simply, without fuss or pretension. I confess, however, to a propensity always to begin at the beginning. There is the bread starter fermenting away at the back of the fridge and some homespun tofu basking in murky water. My wife won't eat that. When my daughter asks for ravioli, I make it from scratch. Come Christmas, I make *pâte de fruits* out of quinces or apples. My wife tears her hair out and tells me to go to a supermarket.

MY MOTHER IS ENGLISH and my father a legal Italian alien. They met in Florence in the 1960s and moved to England to escape Dad's conscription. As a result, my first trip to Italy to meet my family there was without him. Once I had turned two my mother and I flew south to Naples and drove to a town called Bisaccia, in the Campania region. There I met my grandmother for the first time in my new home from home and forever holiday destination, a small working town of a few thousand people, high in the hills, looking down over Puglia. She was the ubiquitous Italian nonna, a lovable tyrant in the kitchen, adept and all-knowing. Lunches on special days began with pasta shaped by her hands and would extend long into the afternoon, finishing with fruit riper than anything I'd known elsewhere. I realise now that these feasts were a product of her ingenuity, for, with little money to spare, her skills in the kitchen could transform the proverbial sow's ear into the silk purse (or pasta).

A communal oven in the town, the *forno*, was used for family baking of all kinds and Nonna explained the multifarious appearance of the bread loaves by telling me that each family used to make their own. Different shapes lasted different lengths of time and families would bake their weekly supply all at once. Nonna herself would carry trays of chicken or rabbit with potatoes on her head to bake on the hearth, and as I grew older, I was entrusted with carrying the precious tray of lunch to the *forno* for roasting.

Italy for me was synonymous with holidays and we would spend six weeks there every summer. Like many Italian families at the time, ours was a big one. We would stop at aunties' and friends' homes on our travels from Canterbury in the family wagon, a Renault 4, driving from Bergamo to Parma, then Florence and finally Campania. I remember perplexingly uncomfortable dining rooms, with hard-backed chairs and cold, tiled floors. But the overriding sense is one of heat: long, sultry, heavy lunches, the dusty, hot streets beyond, sleeping after lunch while the adults topped up their wine glasses with peaches, evening ice creams in the piazza. Through the narrow cobbled streets of Bisaccia, the smell of pungent wild oregano and drying tomatoes would guide even a stranger to the town's excellent bakery. It was the stuff of dreams for the whole long winter we were in England. At Christmas, Nonna would send a big cardboard box full of *caciocavallo*, salami, wheels of pecorino. These lined our pantry along with the racks of sliced, dried mushrooms that a homesick Dad collected in Blean Woods.

All through this time I had no idea that I was going to be a chef. I just kept on eating and experiencing.

OVER THE YEARS, my mother assimilated many of Nonna's classics. This became a sort of cultural exchange as she introduced our Italian cousins to British staples: sponge cake, fruit crumble and the like. Our kitchen in Canterbury was a Little Italy with a table that was seldom set for family alone. School friends competed to sup with us and it was a wonder that Mum could keep up with the demand.

Some of this feeder instinct must have rubbed off on me, as I really enjoyed cooking for friends, and by the time I'd left school it was established that I was the cook among us. My inclination was to bypass further study, but with the encouragement of my parents I applied for, and was accepted on, a politics degree course. During my studies, I discovered restaurant kitchens, which I loved. I worked in Whitstable during the summers, where I found my feet in the kitchen and discovered how good English ingredients could be. My parents went to Italy without us and I longed for the summer in a new way, with money in my pocket and the physical application that provided just the sort of contrast that a sedentary student needed. Alongside the politics set texts on my bookshelves were the likes of Elizabeth David, Claudia Roden and Antonio Carluccio. I had no idea that I might be considered fit for service in any of the places I dreamed of working and, sometimes, having a politics degree seemed a bit of an impediment.

For a year of my degree, I studied in Naples, where I fed my growing obsession. Zio Giulio, my dear uncle, drove down from Florence and took me to one of the excellent local pizzerias, where we consumed two pies each, and I drank treacly espressos and ate chocolate *cornetti* at breakfast. Meanwhile, I earned credentials cooking for my Italian housemates, almost all of whom received weekly food parcels from concerned relatives. Several were pretty handy on our only stove, a Primus, and they taught me how to make things tasty. Lentils with sausage or tuna pasta were the staples because they were cheap and quick. I still love and cook them when the fridge is looking bare.

Somewhere along the line I decided I had to cook professionally and, within a week of graduating, I found myself convincing an Italian restaurant in Covent Garden to give me a trial. I lasted six months but then ended up back in Whitstable, shucking oysters until my hands ached before working my way up the ranks. I was there for a year or so before going to Sydney, where my uncle and aunt live, and falling into a busy Italian kitchen. I worked harder there than I had ever worked in my life. It was a great basis for graduating to the restaurant back in London a year later.

I'VE THOUGHT ABOUT WRITING A BOOK of my own for years. I am reverential of the cookery classics, of the likes of Elizabeth David, Marcella Hazan and Patience Gray, but this reverence translated into stage fright. It preoccupied me how I could be relevant, useful and ultimately standout in a saturated cookery-book market.

And then I found clarity. The cooking that I do at home, today, has become a crystallisation of what I make at work, every day, and what I have eaten, and look forward to eating, whenever I return to Italy. It's food that I want to serve back to the people who inspired it, whether colleagues, or my aunts, uncles and cousins. I would have even risked presenting some of the best dishes to Nonna – well into her nineties when she died, she was finally proud of what she taught me.

I see this book as offering practical, exciting and at times off-beat renditions of familiar classics, plus some new dishes. This is prototypical Italian cooking, updated. It reflects how people shop and cook now, but it is a book that I would willingly show to my more traditional, home-making aunties. The food traditions that I am talking about are, for the most part, popular traditions. They are from places where the same dishes have evolved slowly over time but nevertheless differ from household to household.

This is a book that has a respect for, and understanding of, the DNA of Italian cooking but is not a slave to its prescriptions. It comes from a solid grounding, professional and personal, in The Rules. Yet the collection of recipes is not reverential. It focuses heavily on pasta and vegetables. This is informed by how my family eat and what interests me the most. I use fish and meat as much for seasoning these days, enjoying larger cuts too but irregularly. Partly this harks back to the *cucina povera* tradition that was second nature to my grandmother – the moral and economic obligation to stretch flavour, drawing all the value and goodness from an expensive cut – but today it also ties into a very real concern for sustainability and supply.

This brings us to the shape of a typical Italian meal, which often comprises a more substantial *primo* than *secondo*, the reverse of what people expect. The reason, as above, is that the *primo* was the sustaining element: pasta, rice, polenta. At home, we always have something first to spin out the ceremony. More often than not, this runs simply to a piece of toast with leftovers – lentils, a roast vegetable, a bit of cheese – on top. It is true to say, however, that a two-course meal is becoming less common in Italy. Graze across the sections of the book and put your meal together to suit you and your family or friends.

You will find no formal dessert section in this book, something which is going to be contentious if only in my household, for my wife loves pudding. I am not claiming not to have a sweet tooth. Maybe I'm one of those people who says no when the waiter is taking the pudding order and then grabs a spoon and cadges from their neighbour. Whatever. In my view, ice cream is the best of all sweet things and biscuits are little miracles that should be always available. These are the recipes you'll find within these pages.

This book completes a personal journey. It is about what occupies me in my own kitchen. Homely but not old-fashioned, this is progressive Italian cooking as I see it. I step to the stove as a cook, not a historian or anthropologist. I will look at Italian cooking traditions from an idiosyncratic point of view. With an eye for the unusual and forgotten, I travel a trodden path with a current outlook. Contemporary cooking isn't necessarily newfangled (I don't yet own a Thermomix); for me it is about being simple, clever, sympathetic and creative. At home, gently inventive, I am free to indulge in the warped recreation of a dish long since eaten or imagined. Keeping abreast of how we like to eat today, I am inspired by flavours from the past. As a professional, I know how to skip superfluous steps. One of the oft-asked questions in my day job is, 'What is your vision for this dish?' I have assimilated a precision that allows me to translate this vision to you, the reader. This is a shrewd kind of cooking, open-minded but careful. I hope, immodestly, that it might inform some new ideas of your own.

PASTA
PASTA

PASTA

Pasta is Italian soul food. Wouldn't we all love a brilliant, easy, local pasta joint on our street? The idea of it conjures up stereotypes about Italian hospitality and comfort eating. Pasta can be as delicate as silk, subtle and gentle in both flavour and texture, or rough around the edges from bronze dyes that allow sauce to stick. It can involve a whole morning's rolling and shaping, or days of slowly cooking a sauce that yields in just the right way. Or it can be that quick-fix supper made when you thought the cupboards were bare. Whether making it for instant gratification or as the treat of treats for a bunch of guests, I think you should invest in dedicated pans – I favour a wide, open Italian *padella* with flared sides, good for tossing and worth splashing out on – and employ your finest china.

The most prized ingredients in the world are saved for serving on pasta: white truffles, sea urchins, bottarga, saffron. But pasta's starch, with the addition of some fat, can also bring majesty to potatoes, sardines and cabbage, with a bit of care. Be careful not to overcook, over-sauce, under-toss, make too wet or too dry. And allow the pasta some time to absorb the sauce. As an experiment, leave the lid on a finished pan of pasta for a couple of minutes and see how any surplus liquid magically disappears. It's worth keeping a cup of the pasta's cooking water on standby in case this resting time has left you with too claggy a result.

I don't like to think of myself as a snob but I have no interest in eating bad, or even average, pasta. Like everyone else of my generation, however, this is what I was unwittingly brought up on. Raised on ubiquitous, mass-produced and low-grade wheat and bread, I now look for better. Part of the reason I have made so much fresh pasta in the past is to have control over the *materie prime*, or primary ingredients. There aren't many, of course – flour, water and possibly eggs for richer doughs – but from these few ingredients can be made scores of different shapes.

The types of pasta I have included in this book require no special equipment. They need a bit of practice but very soon get easier to make. I think that using a rolling pin is actually less daunting to the novice than a special machine, but that method does take longer. Neither is as quick as having ready-made; therefore I also recommend finding a good source of slow-dried pasta. It is becoming easier to buy pasta from artisanal producers using better grains, and although fresh orecchiette and ravioli are still firm family favourites, it is the best brands of dried pasta that make up our everyday supply. All the pasta recipes in this book can be made using them.

DRIED PASTA

It's sad but true that for the past few years pasta has become slightly unfashionable, with even some Italians giving it a wide berth. This can be attributed in part to the postwar period, when Italy under the Marshall Plan was won over by modified versions of its *grano duro* (hard wheat) grains. These new cultivars have higher yields and, crucially, grow close to the ground, allowing for mechanised harvesting. These grains became the pasta that was sold to the world, but the gluten in them is less digestible and has contributed to a rise in intolerance and coeliac disease. In contrast, the gluten in ancient wheats has evolved with us over millennia and does not cause digestive problems.

Once again we need to look back to move forwards. Indeed, just as the 'Real Bread' movement – based on the concept of slow, naturally leavened breads, made with organically farmed whole-wheat flour – has swept Europe and America, there is a similar but much quieter movement in pasta circles. Which makes total sense: if whole-wheat flour reduces cholesterol in bread, it also does in pasta; if freshly milled flour tastes great in bread, then it does so in pasta too.

An artisanally manufactured (I dislike that word but here it is appropriate) pasta must be slow-dried at a low temperature, ideally in highish humidity. A big pasta factory can take wheat from flour to packaged product in minutes, but using old-style production this takes days. Something else to be aware of is the way the big players are looking to mimic the branding and looks of the artisan producers. Bronze dyes, for example, make a rough-edged pasta that many people like, including me, but this is not the mark of quality. That relies on the slow processing of good old grain that is high in starch; that is the benchmark. The best pasta is pale, not yellow, a good thing to look out for. And a word about gluten-free pasta. It is the gluten that holds pasta together, and without it a dough cannot be made. Corn, for example, contains no gluten, so artificial products are added to hold corn pasta together; these are unhealthy in a way that ancient glutens are not.

I know this is sounding a bit like a manifesto but I am determined to improve the image of gluten. I don't need to tell you that healthy eating is actually about balance and moderation, and not avoiding something that has looked after us for thousands of years. Gluten for President.

HERE ARE THE DIFFERENT KINDS OF FRESH PASTA YOU WILL FIND WITHIN THE BOOK:

GNOCCHI and dumplings need little introduction. It's best to use as light a touch as possible when making, kneading and shaping. Cooking soon after production is also highly recommended.

ORECCHIETTE is the queen of pasta as far as my family and I are concerned. A classic Sunday lunch treat, they take patience and an early start to shape enough. Called 'little ears' they look more like little hats.

CAVATELLI are the close cousins of orecchiette and they also take their time. Excavated with fingertips, they are thicker and consequently have a pleasing chew to them.

TAGLIATELLE are simple strips. Maybe the most ubiquitous of fresh pasta shapes, it is possible to find them in varying grades. A rich yellow colour is usually a good sign as it means quality eggs have been used in the manufacture. Roll the pasta sheets up, cut them with a knife and then unravel.

QUADRATINI are simple squares cut from a fresh pasta sheet.

PIZZOCCHERI are wider and shorter than tagliatelle. The buckwheat flour means they have to be rolled quite thick and they break into shorter pieces easily.

PICI are the famous thick noodles from central Italy. Think hand-rolled spaghetti.

MARCANALI are similar to pici cut with a grooved rolling pin. This chewy noodle is really good with meat sauces.

FRESH PASTA

The fresh pasta that I have used in this book is mostly thick and hand-shaped. It is possible to make with many different grades of flour; I usually put at least a bit of '00' in the mix but also like to add rougher and more flavoursome flours into the mix.

In all cases, if you are in a hurry or you don't feel like making fresh pasta, dried can be used as a substitute; shop-bought tubes or bow ties or shells for the shorter shapes, and tagliatelle or linguine for the longer – or go completely off-piste and pick whatever you prefer.

The best way to make pasta dough is by hand. I do sometimes start in a food processor; this is particularly useful when adding a vegetable or herb to the dough. Mine is from the 1980s; I care for it little and at best save five minutes' mixing as there is no good substitute to finishing by hand. At worst you'll break your mixer, so I'd go with the satisfaction of doing it manually.

The amount of moisture can really vary. The amounts I give within the recipes are a very good guide but be prepared to make minor adjustments according to the weather, size of egg and type of flour, but don't get too stuck on the right stiffness of the flour. A good kneading is far more important.

There is a very good chance that you already know the method for making a pasta dough. It goes like this:

HOW TO MAKE A BASIC PASTA DOUGH

For 4 people, you'll need roughly 200g semola flour, 200g '00' flour, 200ml water.

Begin by pouring the flour onto the worktop in a mountain. If using two different types, mix them together a bit first before making that shape. It's not necessary to sift.

Turn the mountain into a volcano by making a well in the middle. This is to dam the wet ingredients, so make sure it's large enough and that there is no escape route.

Use a fork to mix the wet ingredients (including eggs if the recipe calls for it) into the flour in a slow whisking-type motion, first just around the border to make a paste, then carry on moving towards the outside of the flour. Very soon the liquid ingredients will be too thick to run away so try to incorporate all the flour into one homogenous dough. It often seems too dry at first but be patient and resist the temptation to add more moisture.

Keep scraping and scratching any pieces of flour sticking to the worktop and cup your hands one over the other. I stick to a strict philosophy of not wasting any flour. I do this by rolling the dough all around the work surface over any stray crumbs.

Once there is a ball of dough, begin to knead. At this stage you might consider whether your dough is too hard or too soft. It will tend to get softer during resting but it is also worth bearing in mind that it is easier to add more flour to a wet dough than vice versa. My grandmother taught me how to add moisture by wetting your hands rather than the dough, kneading that in before wetting them again. This works well but is time-consuming.

I suggest kneading with your strongest hand, pressing into the dough with the base of your palm and away from you, while the other keeps the dough still. Use this spare hand to fold it slightly back towards you as the other turns the dough through 45 degrees. But any good pounding will do. Repeat. And repeat.

Get a rhythm up and use the weight of your body behind the kneading action to help. Udon noodles get trampled on to bring on their gluten development.

The texture and feel of the dough will change. All but the roughest wholemeal flour-based doughs will become smoother and more luxurious. And it will feel increasingly elastic, springy and smooth as the glutens are stretched in every direction. Press your thumb into the dough to check its elasticity – it should be strong enough to spring back into shape.

The pasta now needs resting – 30 minutes is enough time for it to relax. Wrap it well to stop it drying. A barely damp tea towel is good. Leave in a cool place, though I rarely put it in the fridge unless it is far in advance of being used. However, it does keep well in the fridge for several days. Some organic flours might speckle a bit overnight. There is nothing bad about this and you won't notice it when cooked.

Shape the dough by hand or roll it flat (the recipes in this book will direct you on what shape to make). Either way you should re-cover the pasta as you use pieces of it and I recommend only using a small piece at a time as it can dry out quickly.

HOW TO MAKE SHAPES

The best way to roll pasta with a machine is to start with a small piece and put it through several times, folding in half each time before putting it back through. Change its direction of travel each time. Then when it feels smoother, start moving down the notches on the machine, one at a time. When you get halfway, put through twice on the same thickness setting. For extra smoothness, fold it back up and begin the process again, but for the recipes in this book it's not really necessary. Dust with a small amount of flour from time to time.

Rolling pasta with a long rolling pin to make a large sheet is an art, but a small one is not so difficult. Dust with flour and turn it around, applying an even pressure over the whole sheet.

Cut simple shapes by hand. I like an irregularity that gives away the fact that they are homemade. Let the pasta dry for a minute or two before lightly dusting and folding over. Use a large knife to cut into strips for tagliatelle, fettucine, tagliolini, pappardelle, etc., or into small squares for quadratini or large ones for lasagnette.

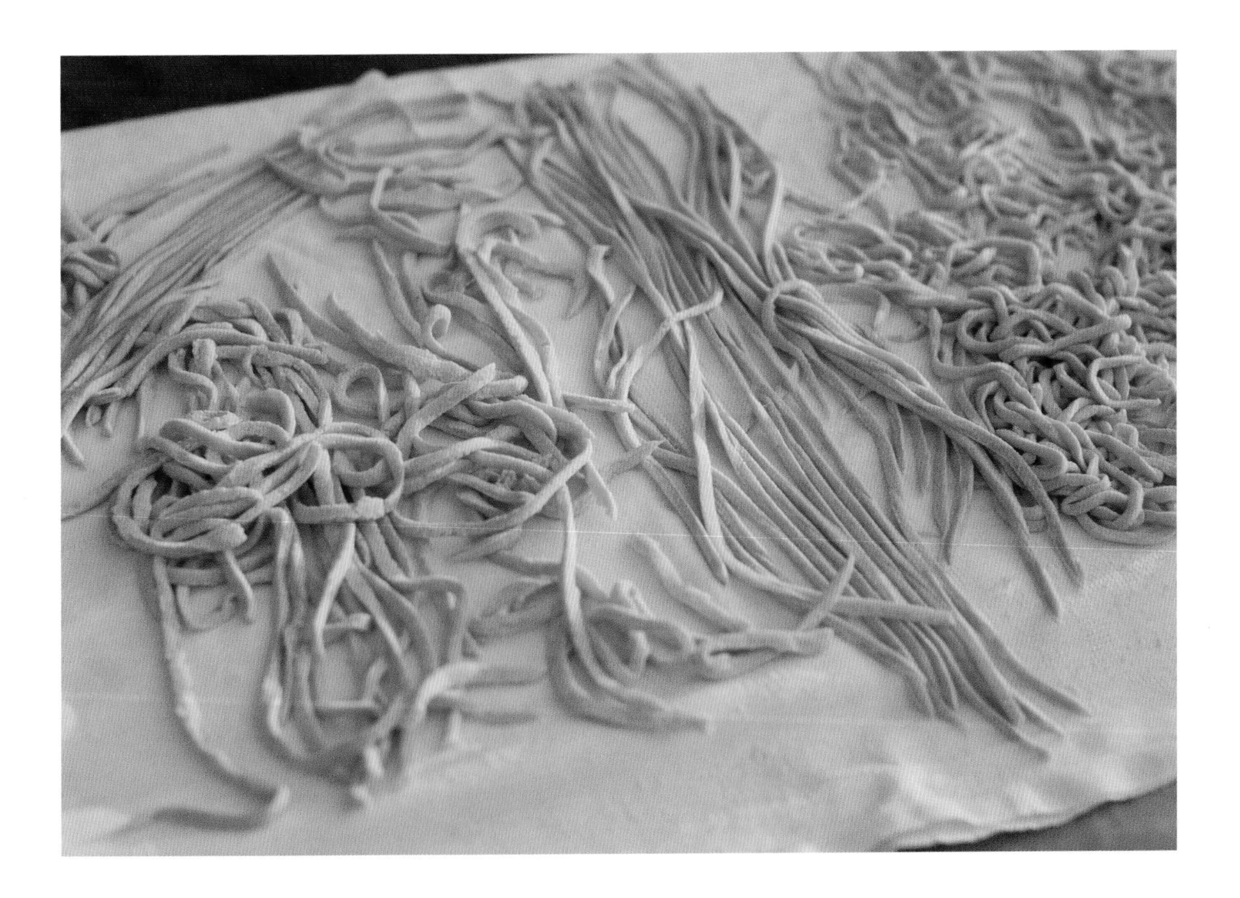

Having eaten a lot of pasta over a long time, I feel my blood pressure rising instinctively whenever the wrong shape is matched with the wrong sauce. It is, for cultural or gourmandising purists, up there with drinking cappuccino after eleven or, even more unforgivably, after lunch. Despite this, I think that much more is made of this than need be, and the truth is that most pasta goes with most things and choice is largely down to personal preference. Most of the sauces herein can be for any sort; take my suggestions as guidance only. The fresh pastas here are rustic and hand-rolled; this doesn't mean that they don't take some perfecting, but they'll be delicious nonetheless.

Sorry about all this prattling on about pasta, but ever since I fell asleep face down in my spaghetti as a child, then awoke only to finish the bowl, it has been an obsession for me.

PENNE WITH BLACK TRUFFLES

PENNE AL TARTUFO NERO

We first had this piled on bruschetta in Abruzzo – unforgettable. There are several types of black truffle, some even grow here, and all are suitable for this dish. Far cheaper than the white variety, they are still a real luxury. This would also be delicious with polenta instead of pasta.

FOR 4

3 salted anchovy fillets

a few parsley sprigs extra finely chopped

1 medium black truffle (about 40g or more)

75g really good unsalted butter at room temperature (the quality makes a difference here)

400g penne

75g grated Parmesan, plus extra to serve

sea salt, black pepper and extra virgin olive oil

Put the anchovies in a small pan and gently heat in 2 tablespoons of olive oil until they melt. Add the parsley and remove from the heat. Grate in almost all the truffle, then add a twist of black pepper and the butter. Mash everything together with the back of a fork.

Boil the pasta in plenty of salted water. When cooked, drain, reserving a cup of the cooking water. Return to the pan, mix first with the Parmesan and then the anchovy-truffle butter, using a little of the cooking water to achieve a creamy consistency. You can do this over a low flame if you are worried about its temperature. Taste for seasoning.

Serve in warm bowls with the remaining truffle and more cheese grated on top.

RIGATONI WITH FIGS

RIGATONI AI FICHI

This sounds like an unusual pairing but actually the faintly spicy figs with the rich cured meat is a delicious combination.

FOR 4

400g rigatoni

150g guanciale or pancetta, sliced

1 tbsp fresh thyme leaves

6 fresh figs, washed and sliced into three

100g grated mature pecorino, plus extra to serve

sea salt, black pepper and extra virgin olive oil

Put a large pan of salted water on to heat. You can start cooking the pasta as soon as it boils as the sauce is that quick to make.

Fry the guanciale or pancetta in a large pan with a tablespoon of olive oil. When it is nice and crispy, and most of the fat has melted, add the thyme and figs and toss quickly.

Drain the pasta, reserving a cup of the cooking liquid. Add the pasta to the other pan and toss everything together, adding the cheese and using the cooking water to emulsify the sauce as necessary. Add a good grind of pepper and salt to taste.

Serve with more cheese for grating at the table.

NOT AMATRICIANA RIGATONI

RIGATONI NON ALL'AMATRICIANA

While a student in Naples in the 1990s, I lived with 14 other young Italian men. On Mondays, they brought back food cooked in their family homes, scattered throughout the region. I longed for Antonio's lentils with sausage or Cesare's mother's clam sauce. As well as these home-cooked treats, we also took turns to cook and everybody had a couple of dishes that were on repeat. One guy from Taranto, I forget his name, taught me to make the sauce he called *Amatriciana*. The very famous pasta sauce from the ill-fated town of Amatrice, I now know, is something different; but this is very good. I saw out my student days back in London, cooking this sauce for other roommates. I like the delicate use of sweet pepper as a seasoning, replacing the onion in the original recipe.

This is the sort of dish that's good eaten on your lap, watching football on a black-and-white telly.

FOR 4

½ yellow pepper, thinly sliced

50g simple pork salami, chopped

2 garlic cloves, sliced

500g best-quality passata or Pommarola (page 100)

400g rigatoni (1kg for student portions!)

grated mature pecorino

sea salt, black pepper and extra virgin olive oil

Put the pepper in a wide pan with 3 tablespoons of olive oil and a pinch of salt and sweat over a medium heat for 5 minutes. Add the salami and garlic and fry for another couple of minutes until the sausage smells good.

Add the passata, bring to a simmer and leave to cook for an hour or more, uncovered, over a low heat. Check it frequently and give a stir to make sure that it's not drying out. Add a splash of water if necessary.

Boil the pasta in plenty of salted water according to the packet instructions. When you drain it, reserve some of the liquid and use it to loosen your sauce to the desired consistency when you stir it together with the pasta. Adjust the seasoning and serve with cheese.

WILD FENNEL SPAGHETTI

SPAGHETTI AL FINOCCHIETTO SELVATICO

This is the best way that I can think of to use that long, stringy fennel with all the fronds attached I see sometimes in the farmers' market. The tough bulbs aren't good for salads or roasting, but their flavour is delicious extracted and used as described in this recipe. Even better may be wild fennel, which grows plentifully along the coastline and country paths.

FOR 4

1 long fennel with fronds

4 dried figs, chopped

1 red onion (preferably Tropea variety) or shallot, sliced

1 garlic clove, roughly chopped

50g pine nuts

½ dried chilli, crushed

400g spaghetti

sea salt, black pepper and extra virgin olive oil

Bring a large pan of salted water to the boil. Cook the fennel whole for 5 minutes or until it begins to soften. Remove the fennel with tongs and set aside, reserving the water to cook the pasta in.

Soften the figs in a ladleful of the warm fennel water until you need them.

Heat 4 tablespoons of olive oil, the onion, garlic and a pinch of salt in a wide pan over a good heat. Add a ladleful of the fennel water and allow to boil for 5 minutes, by which point the water should have evaporated and the onion and garlic will begin to fry again. Season.

Add the pine nuts, chopped figs drained of their water bath, and chilli. Allow to carry on cooking gently while you chop the fennel into fairly thin strips and add to the pan.

Boil the spaghetti in the fennel water. When it is 30 seconds from al dente, drain and add to the sauce, using half a cup or so of its starchy water to help it thicken.

Add extra olive oil and allow to sit for 2 minutes. This is good served without cheese.

RIGATONI WITH YELLOW PEPPERS
RIGATONI CON PEPERONI GIALLI

This is a recipe that uses a lot of sweet pepper whizzed into a smooth sauce. I enjoy the juxtaposition of it with the spicy raw basil: a very satisfying and unusual result from just a few ingredients. Whole-wheat pasta is also a great choice with this sauce.

FOR 4

1 large yellow pepper, deseeded and sliced

2 garlic cloves, thinly sliced

½ dried chilli

40ml double cream

400g whole-wheat rigatoni

bunch basil, leaves only

salted ricotta (optional)

sea salt and extra virgin olive oil

Place a medium pan over a medium-high heat and add 2 tablespoons of olive oil. Fry the pepper for 3 minutes before adding the garlic with a pinch of salt. Crumble in the chilli and continue to cook over a lower heat, stirring occasionally and covering in between. Cook the pepper until completely soft. This might take up to 30 minutes.

Once the pepper is cooked, add the cream and bring to the boil. Simmer, stirring, for 5 minutes. Taste the sauce for seasoning – it should be sweet, rich and spicy.

Purée in a food processor until smooth and return to the pan.

Cook the pasta in plenty of salted water until al dente, following the instructions on the packet. Drain, reserving a cup of the cooking water, and add the pasta to the pan containing the peppers. Toss over a low heat, adding the basil leaves and using the pasta water if necessary to make the sauce creamy and luscious.

Serve on warm plates with grated salted ricotta, if you like.

SPAGHETTONI WITH SALTED SARDINES
SPAGHETTONI CON SARDINE SALATE

Pasta with sardines is a Venetian classic. Bigoli is the thick spaghettoni traditionally made by forcing dough through a *torchio* (pasta press). By hand it is very hard work – much better to buy it already formed. I was taught by a fourth generation *pastaiolo* (pasta maker) that aficionados look to spaghettoni as the benchmark of a good brand. Made with a tasty wheat, it has a satisfyingly moreish chew and is extra starchy, almost self-saucing. I'd love to use that same *pastaiolo*'s excellent whole-wheat version when I make this dish.

It might seem excessive to salt your own sardines but commercial ones are hard to find and, when you do, they are usually under rancid oil. Instead, this salting is quick enough and much cheaper.

FOR 4

12 small sardines, exceptionally fresh

3 tbsp breadcrumbs

2 garlic cloves

1 small red onion, finely sliced

knob of butter

100ml white wine

400g spaghettoni

25g grated Parmesan

sea salt, black pepper and extra virgin olive oil

[1] Pasta press | [2] Pasta maker

Gut the sardines and clean them inside really well. Pay special attention to the blood line that runs under the bones. Rinse, scatter with salt and leave in the fridge. It's that straightforward. One day left in the salt is enough.

The next day, wash the sardines thoroughly and peel the fillets from the bone using your fingers, or fillet with a small knife if you prefer. Peel the skin off too.

Spread the breadcrumbs out in a frying pan with 3 tablespoons of olive oil and a whole garlic clove. Place over a high heat and fry, stirring, until golden and crispy. Remove to a plate lined with kitchen paper and discard the garlic.

Chop the remaining garlic clove. Put the onion with the butter and a glug of olive oil in a saucepan large enough to eventually accommodate the pasta. Add a cup of water and begin to cook over a lowish heat.

When the water has evaporated and the onion softened, add the chopped garlic and fry for 45 seconds before adding the wine. As the wine boils, add the sardine fillets, snipping them in pieces. Cook for a few minutes, stirring to help the fish dissolve. Remove from the heat.

Boil the pasta in salted water for one minute less than stated on the packet. Save a good amount of its starchy water. Add the drained pasta to the saucepan, once again over the heat with a ladle of the cooking water. The pasta will begin to soak up the sauce. Add another splash of water if necessary, plus some Parmesan and a liberal grinding of pepper. Transfer to a serving dish and sprinkle over the breadcrumbs.

CHICKPEA SOUP AND QUADRATINI

ZUPPA DI CECI CON QUADRATINI

This is pretty easy to make with just what you have in the store cupboard – ideal as a midweek dish or for an impromptu Saturday in. You can omit the soaking stage with the chickpeas and just open a can (the cooking process roughly doubles the weight of dried chickpeas). It's really versatile so feel free to use this as a blueprint, experimenting with dried and fresh pasta and the herbs and vegetables you use. The pasta from the Ravioli recipe (page 49) works well.

FOR 4

250g dried chickpeas, soaked overnight in cold water

5 sage sprigs

5 garlic cloves

1 leek, sliced

bunch parsley, leaves and stalks chopped

1 dried red chilli, crumbled

4 anchovies

8 ripe plum tomatoes, fresh or jarred, peeled and chopped, or Pommarola (page 100)

360g fresh pasta

grated Parmesan (optional)

sea salt, black pepper and extra virgin olive oil

Drain the chickpeas and put in a pan with the sage and 3 of the garlic cloves. Cover with water and boil until tender, roughly an hour. Drain, reserving the cooking liquid.

In a saucepan, sweat the leek with the remaining garlic and the parsley stalks in a little olive oil. When really soft, add the chilli and anchovies and, when they have melted, the tomatoes and cooked chickpeas. Cook until the tomatoes have thoroughly broken down (this will take longer if using canned) and adjust the seasoning. Then cover with the reserved chickpea water and, once hot, encourage the chickpeas to break up a bit. You can help them along by crushing with the back of a spoon or whizzing smoother if you prefer.

Boil the pasta in plenty of salted water. While the pasta is cooking, which if you're using fresh will take no time, put the chickpeas into one large warmed serving dish, or individual bowls, and then place the drained pasta on top, sprinkling with the chopped parsley leaves, a drizzle of oil and freshly grated cheese if required.

CAVATELLI PASTA WITH CHICKPEAS

CAVATELLI E CECI

I cannot resist another quick *pasta e ceci*, sorry.

FOR 4

250g chickpeas, soaked overnight in cold water

5 sage sprigs

4 garlic cloves

1 rosemary sprig

100g bresaola, cut into strips

350ml light meat stock

1 quantity fresh cavatelli (see page 80)

grated Parmesan

sea salt, black pepper and extra virgin olive oil

Drain the chickpeas and put in a pan with the sage and 3 of the garlic cloves. Cover with water and boil until tender, roughly an hour.

Chop the remaining garlic clove and rosemary together until fine. Put in a pan with the bresaola and a little oil and place over a moderate heat. When you can smell the rosemary, add the drained cooked chickpeas and the stock. Bring to the boil and then simmer for 20 minutes.

Cook the pasta in a pan of boiling salted water. When nearly cooked, scoop out using tongs straight into the chickpeas and allow to finish cooking off the heat. Taste and adjust the seasoning.

Serve with *olio buono* (good oil), plenty of black pepper and Parmesan.

SPAGHETTONI WITH ALMONDS AND GREEN PEPPERS

SPAGHETTONI CON MANDORLE E PEPERONI VERDI

The idea for this sauce came from a meal a friend ate in Amalfi, where they have 'sweet' peppers called *friggitelli*. Closer to home, I find it easier to buy either Padrón peppers or longer pale green Turkish peppers. Either is fine here, the Spanish ones having a nice heat, but avoid the big dark green monstrosities that used to be a feature of pub salads.

FOR 4

200g long green peppers

¼ garlic clove

35g shelled fresh almonds, or dried almonds soaked in water overnight and then peeled

small bunch parsley, or a mix of parsley and marjoram

50g grated salted ricotta or salty pecorino Romano

400g spaghettoni

sea salt, black pepper and extra virgin olive oil

Carefully burn the whole peppers over a naked gas flame using tongs. If you don't cook on gas it's probably not worth lighting the barbecue for this; instead, sear them in a hot dry pan, or in the oven. Turn the peppers when they are blackened but don't worry about getting them done on all sides as you would if you were going to peel them.

When they are done, put them in a bowl and cover with cling film until they are cool enough to handle. Roughly rub off the loosest of the black skin, remove the inedible tops, and place in a blender with the garlic, almonds and parsley.

Whizz, adding a spoonful or more of water as necessary while it's moving. When smoothish, add the cheese and an extra good glug of oil and buzz one more time to combine, then check the seasoning.

Cook the spaghetti until al dente, drain and dress with the sauce, using a ladleful of the cooking water to loosen.

ORECCHIETTE WITH NEW OIL

ORECCHIETTE ALL'OLIO NUOVO

When I asked my then teenaged cousin, Leonardo, what his favourite pasta was, he said, without skipping a beat, that it was fresh orecchiette with new oil and salted ricotta. If you are lucky enough to have the latest new pressing of organic oil, no more than a few months old, this is a good way to use it. At other times of the year, a simple tomato sauce with salted ricotta is a firm favourite. Making your own orecchiette is a labour of love, one best reserved for high days and holidays. That said, if there's a fresh pasta worth the effort of making just for you, it would probably be this one.

FOR 6

80g spelt flour, or extra semola flour

120g semola flour

200g 'oo' flour

200ml water

75ml fresh olive oil

200g salted ricotta, finely grated

sea salt

Make a dough as described on page 25 but using the flours and water listed here, and rest for at least half an hour. Once rested, take a large walnut-sized piece of pasta and roll with uniform pressure into a cylinder on a clean worktop using the palms of your hands. You can use a light dusting of flour but don't throw it around too much as friction on the worktop will be necessary next.

When you have a sausage of dough about 1cm thick, cut it into pieces about 1cm long. These can be bigger if you'd prefer a larger pasta or have large thumbs. Now you want to shape the dough pieces into the 'little ears' the pasta is named after. Place a butter knife on to a piece leaving the cutting edge facing away from you and at its top. Pull it towards you, pressing quite hard as you do so. Stretch the dough around the tip of the knife. I recommend pressing too hard on purpose at first and then applying less pressure over subsequent attempts until you get the hang of it. You should end up with a sort of pasta shell stuck to the end of your knife. Invert this onto your thumb to make the dome of a 'little ear'. Place the orecchiette one by one on a tray lined with a clean towel in a celebration of your effort and leave them to dry. Practice makes perfect; it takes a few tries but isn't as hard as it seems. If you are making a lot do it in company, and if you are really struggling an online video might also help.

When ready, cook the orecchiette in well-salted boiling water for 5 minutes until they float. If you're unsure they are done, eat one to test. Place a generous amount of pasta in each serving bowl and cover with the oil and a heap of grated ricotta. Everybody enjoys mixing their own.

SALTED RICOTTA AND CACIORICOTTA | RICOTTA SALATA E CACIORICOTTA

I'm not sure that *ricotta salata* and *cacioricotta* would give your average *Maître Fromager* much to get excited about. They aren't technically even cheeses. However, they taste absolutely of milk and are ubiquitous in southern Italy and a fixture in the home kitchen. Grated or flaked, they lend a healthy piquancy and creaminess to green vegetables and give a welcome zing to tomato salad, matching perfectly with my default dressing of marjoram and extra virgin olive oil.

Ricotta salata is a lightly salted pressed ricotta matured for at least ninety days. It can also be made with goat or ewe's milk. This is something I think it worthwhile to pick up when I'm on holiday in Italy and bring back with me. It lasts well kept wrapped in cloth; but when it's finished, I look for cow or sheep *cacioricotta* – a halfway house between cheese and ricotta that uses whole milk instead of whey and contains rennet. It can be found in specialist shops and Italian delis (if your local delicatessen doesn't stock it, you could always ask them if they know a supplier). Both *ricotta salata* and *cacioricotta* are chalky and firm in character and can be used interchangeably.

The plain recooked whey, ricotta, is popular for justifiable reasons. From the top window of my parents' apartment in Radicondoli, you can see sheep grazing at a farm in nearby Belforte. Here they produce miraculous fresh and aged cheeses, as well as yoghurt so creamily delicious as to make you feel really excited about breakfast. The fresh ricotta is irresistible in savoury or sweet dishes, baked or just as it is, spooned over tomatoes, salad leaves, pasta or fresh fruit. The stuff you can buy in tubs in a supermarket needs a bit more treatment before it can hold up to the excellence of this local product. But I use it anyway for cakes, puddings and pancakes as well as in sauces and baked egg dishes: a truly versatile ingredient.

RAVIOLI
CAUZUNGIEDD

In her dialect, Nonna called ravioli *cauzungiedd*. Impossible to pronounce but this is what I order for my birthday again now that Dad has taken on her mantle as chief *Raviolo*. It is more down to earth than, say, the divine filled pasta of Bologna. What I especially appreciate is the taste of parsley in the ricotta.

FOR 8

2 garlic cloves, finely sliced

1 chilli, crushed

3 basil leaves (optional)

800g passata or Pommarola (page 100)

350g '00' flour

350g semola flour, plus extra for dusting

280ml water

2–3 eggs

4 parsley sprigs, chopped

1kg ricotta, preferably sheep's

salted ricotta or mature hard pecorino, grated

sea salt and extra virgin olive oil

To make a simple tomato sauce, heat 2 tablespoons of olive oil in a pan and fry the garlic with a pinch of salt. When opaque add the chilli, basil and passata and simmer over a low heat until well cooked and transformed – you want it thicker, deeper in colour and full of flavour.

Make a dough as described on page 25 using the flours, water and 2 of the eggs listed here. While it's resting, make the filling.

Mix the parsley into the ricotta with a fork and a pinch of salt. My grandmother told me that if the ricotta is not up to her standard she adds an egg. I almost always add one. Cover a large board with a tea towel and lightly flour with semola, then set aside.

To assemble the ravioli, cut off a double walnut-sized piece of dough. Roll out with a long rolling pin or using a pasta machine. Roll to about 2mm thick, that is to say thin but not paper thin. If you are using a pasta machine, adjust the thickness setting to about halfway.

Place a teaspoon of the ricotta mix along the length of the pasta at 6cm intervals. Do this as cleanly as possible. If you get ricotta everywhere the pasta will not stick shut. Very slightly wet the pasta to one side of the ricotta using a brush or your finger dipped in a glass of water. Fold the top over the bottom. Press down around the ricotta between the parcels, working from one end to the other. Try to ensure there is as little air trapped inside as possible.

Using a butter knife or pasta wheel, cut around the three sides of the ravioli, trimming a couple of centimetres away from the filling but keeping all the little off-cuts of dough. Transfer the individual ravioli to the towelled board. Store somewhere cool until needed and not for so long that they adhere to the cloth – you should use them on the day you make them.

continued >

When you are ready to eat, get everyone to the table as the pasta cooks quickly. Boil in salted water for about 5 minutes with all the little trimmings. It is less risky to remove the pasta to a warm plate with a slotted spoon or spider rather than drain in a colander.

Serve with the tomato sauce and pass the grated cheese around.

CHESTNUT FLOUR TAGLIATELLE AND BROAD BEANS

TAGLIATELLE DI CASTAGNE CON FAVE SECCHE

Rustic sweet pasta pairs well with earthy dried broad beans. Don't forget to soak the broad beans overnight. This will loosen their tough outer coating and enable you – if they are not already podded – to squeeze them from their skins. I usually soak and cook more than I need as I enjoy having them ready to eat with olive oil. Nutritious, delicious.

FOR 4

160g chestnut flour

250g 'oo' flour

70ml water

2 eggs

100g dried broad beans, soaked overnight in cold water

2 garlic cloves

4 bay leaves

small bunch parsley

10 green olives, pitted and chopped

100g soft sheep's cheese

40g pecorino, grated

sea salt, black pepper and extra virgin olive oil

Make a dough as described on page 25 using the flours, water and eggs listed here – you will end up with a dough that is caffé latte-coloured. Once rested, roll the dough out using either a long rolling pin or a pasta machine, but don't make it too thin – keep it a couple of millimetres thick. If you are using a pasta machine, adjust the thickness setting to about halfway. Allow to dry a little, roll up and cut into tagliatelle 1cm in width.

Drain the broad beans. Put them in a saucepan with the garlic and bay leaves and cover with fresh water approximately 6cm above the beans. Simmer until soft – this will take about 40 minutes. Add more water if necessary. Then turn up the heat, remove the bay leaves and carry on cooking until the beans are thickened and crushed. Once the water has mostly gone, begin to stir. You can do this over a high heat if you stir continuously. I enjoy the cracking sound the edges of the pan make while you move the contents around.

Chop most of the parsley and add to the beans with the olives, a glug of olive oil and the soft cheese. Season with salt and pepper to taste. Stir to combine.

Cook the pasta in plenty of boiling salted water for a few minutes. Then drain, reserving a cup of cooking water to loosen the sauce if necessary, and gently toss the pasta in the sauce.

Serve with extra oil, the grated pecorino and some reserved parsley leaves for effect.

CHESTNUT FLOUR TAGLIATELLE WITH SAUSAGE, LEEKS AND SAGE

TAGLIATELLE DI CASTAGNE CON SALSICCIA, PORRO E SALVIA

It is just beginning to get easier to find good sausages made in the UK, by which I mean with pork only, no added rusk or anything. When I have them properly made and slightly aged, sausage is a favourite of mine. This recipe mitigates for not having them. This is what I have been doing for a long time, using a little bit of something cured to achieve an aged sausage flavour.

This dish is most interesting when eaten with the tagliatelle from the previous recipe.

FOR 4

250g Italian pork sausages (100 per cent pork meat),

or:

- **200g pork shoulder, coarsely minced**
- **50g pancetta or other cured meat, minced or finely chopped**
- **1 garlic clove, finely chopped**
- **1 tbsp fennel seeds**

2 leeks, chopped into 2cm discs

12 sage leaves

200ml white wine

zest of 1 lemon

1 quantity fresh Chestnut Flour Tagliatelle (page 52)

50g Parmesan, grated

sea salt, black pepper and extra virgin olive oil

If you are making your own sausage meat, combine the fresh and cured meats in a large mixing bowl with the garlic and a good sprinkling of salt. Add a generous pinch of freshly cracked black pepper and the fennel seeds and mix everything together. Then transfer to a clean surface and continue to mix and press with the palm of your hand to make sausage meat. If you are using shop-bought sausages, just open them with a knife and remove the meat therein.

Heat 2 tablespoons of oil in a wide pan and add the sausage meat by flaking it in with your fingertips. Add the leeks and sage at the same time and fry, stirring, for about 8 minutes. Pour over the wine, cover and cook on the lowest heat for about 1 hour until the meat is completely yielding. Grate in the zest of the lemon.

Cook the tagliatelle in boiling salted water for 5 minutes and then drain, reserving a cup of the cooking liquid for the sauce. Toss, using the cooking water if required, and serve with the Parmesan.

PUMPKIN GNOCCHI AND CHICKEN LIVERS
GNOCCHI DI ZUCCA CON FEGATELLI

These gnocchi are best with a dry, sweet pumpkin. Butternuts don't tend to work as well. The Japanese kabocha squash (or the similar delica in Italian) works well, as do blue-skinned varieties like crown prince.

FOR 4

400g floury potatoes, scrubbed

450g pumpkin, peeled and cut into 4cm slices

10g sea salt

150g '00' flour, plus extra

1 egg

nutmeg

150g chicken livers

½ garlic clove, sliced

½ dried chilli, crushed

1 marjoram sprig, leaves only

50ml cheap brandy

3 tablespoons Pommarola (page 100; or ready-made)

300ml meat stock (any type)

50g Parmesan, grated

sea salt, black pepper and extra virgin olive oil

Preheat the oven to 180°C/fan 160°C/gas 4.

To make the gnocchi, bake the potatoes whole until completely cooked. Place the pumpkin slices side by side in a tin lined with baking paper and cook for about 20 minutes – don't cover them as the idea is to dry them as much as possible, but don't let them colour either. Once the potatoes and pumpkin are cooked, work swiftly. The best gnocchi are made with warm ingredients. Remove the skins and mash everything with a potato ricer or food mill (mouli) – not in a processor.

In a separate bowl, mix the salt with the flour. Dust a clean surface with half of the salted flour and put the mash on top, followed by the egg (but omit if the vegetables are excessively moist), the rest of the flour and a good grating of nutmeg.

With both your hands open like shovels, fold the mixture in on itself from the edges and then top and bottom. Keep moving it until you have a dough. You may need more flour if your vegetables are moist.

Take a fist-sized piece of dough and, using your palms, roll on the worktop into a thick sausage, about 2cm in diameter. Use a butter knife to cut them into cylinders 2cm long. Dust with a little flour as needed and move to a board lined with a clean tea towel also dusted with flour.

Clean the chicken livers, cutting out any sinew and anything else untoward. Chop into rough pieces.

Heat a tablespoon of oil in a pan and add the garlic. When translucent, add the chilli, marjoram leaves and livers with a pinch of salt. Brown the meat all over and deglaze with the brandy. Add the pomarola and stock and cook over a low heat for 20 minutes.

Cook the gnocchi in a saucepan of boiling water for 3 minutes, drain and add to the livers for another 2 minutes to finish cooking.

Serve with Parmesan.

OVEN-BAKED PASTA DONATO-STYLE

PASTA AL FORNO DONATO

This pasta is the invention of Donato – a barman friend – and involves the use of a leftover soup. I love it, as it's a melting pot of influences; cabbage and potatoes are a northern combination but prepared in southern style.

FOR 6

1 savoy cabbage, or similar

½ red onion, sliced

2 garlic cloves

3 baking potatoes, peeled and halved

1 ripe plum tomato, fresh or jarred, or 2 tbsp Pommarola (page 100)

1 celery stick, preferably with a few leaves, roughly chopped

500g conchiglioni (large shell-shaped pasta)

250g scamorza, cubed

100g grated Parmesan, plus a little piece of rind

sea salt, black pepper and extra virgin olive oil

Chop the cabbage into quarters and cut out the heart, allowing the leaves to fall into the sink to be washed. If the heart looks exceptionally nice, then trim it and include.

Sweat the onion in a large ovenproof dish with 2 tablespoons of olive oil and the garlic. Once soft, add the Parmesan rind, then the potato halves, tomato and celery. Stir, add the cabbage and just enough water to cover. Bring to the boil, cover with a lid and simmer until the cabbage is collapsingly soft and the potatoes can be easily broken into pieces with a fork. This will take around 50 minutes on a low heat with the lid on.

Then preheat the oven to 190°C/fan 170°C/gas 5.

In a separate pan of boiling salted water, cook the pasta for 5 minutes less than stated on the packet. Drain the pasta and mix with the 'soup'. Add a thin stream of oil and the cheeses, then stir and bake in the oven for 20 minutes, uncovered. It should emerge golden and bubbling.

SPELT FLOUR PICI WITH MILD GARLIC

PICI DI FARRO ALL'AGLIONE

Juvenile spring garlic was recently delivered in my veg box without my asking, so fresh and full of promise and dropped onto the doorstep in Shepherd's Bush – absolutely magic. Trying to be fashionable, I was all set to pickle it when something pricked my conscience and instead I made this version of a Tuscan classic. *Aglione* – a very large but mild type of garlic that was prevalent in Tuscany – would traditionally have been used for this recipe, but while my British bulbs were pretty small and regular, they did not have a strong flavour and suited this dish well.

Good brands of dry pici or thick spaghettoni are possible substitutes for the fresh pasta.

FOR 4

150g spelt flour

150g '00' flour, plus extra for dusting

130ml water

3 small spring garlic bulbs (you could use 20g wild garlic instead), peeled and halved

1 celery stick, cut into three pieces

5 ripe tomatoes, peeled, or 200g canned Italian tomatoes drained of their juices or Pommarola (page 100)

200ml red wine

½ dried chilli

sea salt, black pepper and extra virgin olive oil

Mix the flours, water and 10ml olive oil listed here together to make a dough as described on page 25.

Once rested, roll out with a rolling pin to about 5mm thick, dusting with flour and turning between rolls. Don't worry too much about its shape. Let it dry for a few minutes before cutting with a knife into 'pici': about as wide as it is thick. Take each picio and roll it with your hands on the work surface to make them rounded. You can decide how long you'd like them. Dust with a little extra flour to stop them sticking together and set them side by side on a floured cloth or tray to dry.

To make the sauce, put the garlic, celery, chilli and tomatoes in a wide pan along with the red wine and bring to the boil. Add a good pinch of salt and then turn down to a simmer for 1 hour. The pan will probably dry up, so do loosen the sauce with a little water if need be.

After an hour, everything should be soft enough to mash with a fork, but if not then remove the solids, chop them a bit and return to the pan, turning the heat down low.

Cook the pasta in plenty of boiling salted water until about three-quarters cooked. This will be just 3 minutes if you've made it fresh, otherwise according to the instructions on the packet. Drain the pici, reserving a ladleful of cooking water, then add to the pan of sauce and finish cooking, stirring continuously. Use the reserved cooking water if necessary – the sauce should be luscious and thick. Add a lot of *olio buono* (good oil) and season with salt and pepper.

BUCATINI WITH CUTTLEFISH

BUCATINI CON SEPPIA

Bucatini, hollow spaghetti-like pasta, really suits this dish but it must be the very hardest pasta to eat. Unruly on the plate, it's a risky business dressing bucatini with ink (optional) so watch out. It's tricky and messy to clean cuttlefish. My advice is to ask your fishmonger to do it for you. Have them reserve the sack separately from the body. You can make this with squid instead if you can't find cuttlefish; it will just cook more quickly.

The freshness and vibrancy of the tomatoes contrast well.

FOR 4

1kg cuttlefish, with or without ink sack

2 garlic cloves, chopped

1 tsp fennel seeds

1 dried chilli, crumbled

175ml dry white wine

300g cherry tomatoes (yellow if you can find them)

small bunch basil, leaves torn

350g bucatini

50g toasted salted almonds, chopped

sea salt and extra virgin olive oil

Slice the cuttlefish roughly the same width as the pasta.

Place the garlic into a cold wide pan with 2 tablespoons of olive oil, the cuttlefish, fennel seeds and chilli. Cover and place over a high heat. When you notice a garlicky aroma, uncover and pour in the wine. Bring to a simmer, cover and allow to cook on a medium heat until the cuttlefish is soft – around 30 minutes. Add a splash of water if it looks like it's catching.

Check the cuttlefish is done by either eating a small piece, or seeing if it pierces easily with a fork. Add the ink from the sack if you are using it; to do this, cut the sack with a knife and then squeeze in. I do this wearing gloves as it's hard to wash off. Allow to cook for 5 minutes more then turn off the heat.

While the cuttlefish is cooking, squeeze and tear the tomatoes with your hands over and into a bowl, season, add torn basil leaves and some olive oil.

Boil the bucatini in plenty of salted water, drain and toss into the cuttlefish. Add the raw tomatoes and allow everything to come together in the pan back over a low heat.

Serve in warm bowls with the almonds scattered over.

GREEN PASTA AND BEANS

PASTA VERDE E FAGIOLI

Arguably the most ubiquitous of all Italian food, there are infinite recipes for *pasta e fagioli*. Here it is with fresh pasta, but for a starchier, creamier result replace with 300g short dried pasta and cook for longer.

Buy beans with a long shelf life. Look for the name of a producer, and try all the different types. When we haven't prepared, like the rest of the sensible world we resort to jars of beans rather than dried. But if you're more organised than me, cook lots and freeze them for later use as Mum does.

FOR 4

150g dried cannellini or other white beans, soaked overnight in plenty of cold water

6 garlic cloves

parsley sprigs

100g spinach, chard or nettles

100g semola flour

100g 'oo' flour

80ml water

1 small onion, chopped

2 celery sticks, chopped

1 dried chilli, crushed

basil leaves

Parmesan or other hard cheese, grated (optional)

sea salt and extra virgin olive oil

Drain the beans, rinse and put in a large pan. Cover with fresh water and add 4 of the garlic cloves and the parsley. Bring to the boil and simmer for about an hour until the beans are cooked. Purée roughly one-quarter of the beans in a food processor before returning to the others.

For the pasta, boil the greens for 5 minutes and run them under the tap to cool. Squeeze out the moisture and blitz finely. Add the semola flour to your mixer and blend. Add the other flour to the mixer and the water and pulse before moving to a board and kneading with your hands for 8 minutes, turning the pasta through 90 degrees regularly. When smooth, cover with a clean tea towel and leave to rest for 30 minutes.

Cut a small walnut-sized – very roughly 50g – chunk of pasta. Place on a large wooden board or directly on the work surface. Roll into a sausage just under 1cm in diameter. Cut this into roughly bean-sized cylinders.

Place a finger on the top part of a cylinder, press down and roll towards you at the same time. This should make a cavatello that curls around your finger which you can flick away to the back of your immediate work space before attempting the next. The centre will have been hollowed out but the edges should still be quite thick, and potentially nicely chewy. Transfer them to a floured and tea towel-lined board and allow to dry for at least an hour.

continued >

Chop the remaining garlic cloves and sweat with the onion, celery and chilli in 2 tablespoons of oil. Do this carefully over a low heat so that the end result is as pale as possible.

Add the puréed beans to the *soffritto* (vegetable base) with the basil leaves and the rest of the beans, and top up with water. I prefer this thicker so err on the side of caution and don't add too much water at first, but keep the kettle boiled and add more when necessary. If you use dried pasta it takes a lot more liquid. Boil everything for 5 minutes before adding the pasta and cooking for 8 minutes more.

Serve with *olio buono* (good oil) and cheese if you must.

ZITI WITH AUBERGINE, PEPPERS, TUNA AND RICOTTA

ZITI MELANZANE, PEPERONI, TONNO E RICOTTA

Ziti are short thin pasta tubes – make this with any short pasta. The sauce has a strong, distinctive taste which is tempered by the ricotta and top notes of the mint. Paying careful attention to the vegetables will transform them into a really special sauce.

FOR 4

1 aubergine (500g-ish)

1 garlic clove

75g canned tuna

½ dried chilli

20 capers

250g small green peppers (Padrón could do), roughly deseeded and chopped

400g ziti

150g fresh ricotta

garden mint (or wild mint if you can find it)

zest of 1 lemon

sea salt, black pepper and extra virgin olive oil

Peel the aubergine and slice into 1cm discs, and then again across to make chips. Put them in a colander with a good pinch of salt and leave to drain in the sink with a plate on top for 30 minutes. Rinse well and pat dry.

Heat 4 tablespoons of oil in a wide pan with the whole garlic clove over a medium heat. Fry until the garlic turns a deep golden colour, then discard it, replacing with the tuna. Break this up as much as possible with the back of a wooden spoon. Fry for a minute so that the oil takes on the flavour of the tuna, then add the chilli, capers and chopped peppers.

Keep cooking, moving every so often, for about 5 minutes before adding the aubergine. Cook for another 5 minutes, then cover and turn down the heat to low.

Cook the pasta and 2 minutes before it's ready, according to the timing on the packet, add a ladleful of the pasta water to the sauce. Drain the pasta, saving another ladleful of cooking water just in case, add to the sauce and continue to turn it over a low heat until everything is well coated.

Add the ricotta and adjust the seasoning. At this point I like to add wild mint, but in its absence I'll settle for a few torn leaves of regular garden mint and a scratch of lemon zest.

PASTA WITH BEANS AND MUSSELS

PASTA E FAGIOLI ALLE COZZE

In our household we eat a lot of pasta with beans. Thus I include more than one variation for you to try at home.

FOR 4

1kg mussels

150g dried borlotti, soaked overnight in cold water, or 300g fresh (or other beans of choice)

5 garlic cloves

1 celery stick, peeled and cut into several pieces

1 ripe tomato, halved

75ml dry white wine

small bunch parsley, chopped

1 dried chilli

2 anchovy fillets

200g tubetti pasta

sea salt and extra virgin olive oil

Clean the mussels as for *Spaghetti alle Vongole* (page 83), removing their beards with a knife as you do so.

Drain the beans and put them in a large pan with all but one garlic clove. Add the celery and tomato. Cover by 6cm with water, adding a little oil too, and bring to the boil. Simmer until cooked, 40 minutes or more.

While the beans are cooking, open the mussels by placing in a sizzling-hot pan with a tablespoon of oil, followed by the wine. Cover with a well-fitting lid. Shake the pan and cook over a high heat until all the mussels have opened, but not excessively long as this will toughen them. Drain into a colander over a bowl to catch the juice. Pick the meat from the shells (discarding any mussels that have refused to open) and sieve and retain any juice.

When the borlotti are cooked, chop the remaining garlic clove. In another large pan, heat 2 tablespoons of oil, add the garlic, most of the parsley and the chilli and fry for 1 minute before adding the anchovy fillets. As soon as they have melted, pour over the mussel juice and boil. Then add the borlotti with their liquid, then the pasta.

You will have to keep an eye on how much liquid the pasta requires, adding more hot water when necessary (cold will disrupt and slow the cooking time). Stir continually so that the pasta doesn't stick to the bottom.

The idea is to cook the pasta to an even consistency. When the pasta is al dente, turn off the heat, add the rest of the chopped parsley and the mussels. Check the seasoning, cover with a lid and let it sit for 5 minutes before serving in warmed bowls.

MARCANNALI WITH ARTICHOKES AND LAMB

MARCANNALI CARCIOFI E AGNELLO

This is a spring dish that I enjoy when made with lamb. A more mature animal would lend itself well to slow-cooking, but I find the flavour a little strong for pasta. Use some shoulder or shank if you can't get neck; just trim the fat first. This is also delicious made with kid or rabbit.

Marcannali are made with the ridged rolling pin often found in speciality cooking shops, but I reckon no one ever uses. I bet there are loads of them looking nice all over the place – now is the time to use one if you find it! You could substitute pici, tagliatelle or any dried pasta that you have to hand.

FOR 4

200g semola flour, plus extra for dusting

200g '00' flour

160ml water

1 egg

200g lamb neck

½ red onion, thinly sliced

2 garlic cloves, thinly sliced

1 celery stick, thinly sliced, plus a few leaves

5 bay leaves

1 thyme sprig

175ml dry wine (any type)

4 medium artichokes

grated pecorino or salted ricotta, or, better still, both

chopped fresh parsley

sea salt, black pepper and extra virgin olive oil

Combine the flours, water and egg listed here to make a dough as described on page 25.

Once rested, take a small piece of dough, roughly golf ball-sized, and flatten gently with the palm of your hand. Flour a board and the dough well and begin to roll, without turning, so that the dough is elongated. When it's about 2cm thick move to the bottom of the board. Take the *marcannalo* (the fancy ridged rolling pin, if you managed to find one) and roll onto the dough from near the bottom, but not the very edge, and roll up the dough, pressing hard. This will both stretch the dough out and cut it at the same time.

Then move the *marcannalo* to the bottom of the piece of dough, carefully align the groves and finish the job by pulling it down towards you. Dusting with yet more flour, hold the dough up and divide the individual pieces. A good trick is to use something not too heavy to weigh down the dough at the bottom for the first roll – your other rolling pin for example. Repeat until all the pasta is used.

Chop the lamb into small pieces and then rock your knife over it, chopping some more to make an exceptionally rough mince. Put the onion, garlic and celery in a large pan and sweat in 3 tablespoons of olive oil. After 8 minutes, when the vegetables are translucent, season and add the lamb and cook gently for another 5 minutes. Before the vegetables brown too much, add the bay, thyme and wine and begin to simmer. The meat will take about 40 minutes to be rendered tender. Use this time to calmly clean (see page 131) and then slice the artichokes. Once the lamb is tender, add the artichokes to the hot pan and cook for a few minutes only before turning off the heat, leaving the pan covered.

Cook the pasta in a pan of boiling salted water for 5 minutes. Drain (reserve some of the cooking water) and toss together with the lamb. Use a little of the reserved pasta water to make it creamy. Serve with the grated cheese and chopped fresh parsley.

PASTA WITH PINE NUTS AND RICOTTA

PASTA CON PINOLI E RICOTTA

I really wanted to include a recipe with tomato and fresh ricotta as it's my dad's favourite. It's the careful cooking of the pine nuts at the start of this summer recipe that enhances their flavour and makes for a special dish. I was going to specify but any short pasta like penne, ziti or fusilli would work well.

FOR 4

3 garlic cloves

⅓ dried chilli

60g pine nuts

300g tomatoes (yellow if you can find them), peeled and chopped

3 basil sprigs

400g short pasta

200g sheep's or cow's ricotta

50g grated pecorino

sea salt, black pepper and extra virgin olive oil

Put the garlic in a wide saucepan with 3 good tablespoons of oil and place over a medium heat. When the garlic begins to turn golden, add the chilli, crumbling a little between your fingers (don't rub your eyes before washing your hands).Turn the temperature down low, remove the garlic and add the pine nuts. Watch them carefully as they cook – don't let them burn.

Add the tomatoes and basil sprigs, and season. When it starts to boil turn down to a simmer and cook for 15 minutes.

Cook the pasta in plenty of salted water until al dente. When draining, reserve a cup of the starchy cooking water.

Toss the pasta into the pan with the sauce and stir. Add the ricotta, half of the pecorino and a spoonful or two of cooking water to achieve the desired consistency. Keep turning over. If it looks dry, a spoonful of olive oil or a little more cooking water could be welcome. Keep turning over.

Serve in warm bowls with the rest of the cheese.

PICI WITH NDUJA AND BREADCRUMBS

PICI E NDUJA CALABRESE CON BRICIOLE

This recipe, and the method I use for making pici with a little oil, comes from a friend called Zach, who hails from a densely wooded, mountainous area of Tuscany. I love the texture of pici made this way. Pici with breadcrumbs is a classic that Zach would have grown up with, but I really like his addition of something good from the south. Nduja is the rich, red, soft sausage from Calabria that's now relatively easy to find in the UK.

A word about breadcrumbs: they should be ground well and dried, and not overly greasy. Having been chastised by my grandmother for throwing away old bread, I always have some to hand.

FOR 4

150g old bread, blitzed to crumbs
2 garlic cloves
1 quantity fresh pici (page 57)
200g soft Calabrian nduja
1 tbsp marjoram leaves
sea salt and extra virgin olive oil

Spread the breadcrumbs out in a frying pan with 3 tablespoons of olive oil and a whole garlic clove. Place over a high heat and fry, stirring, until golden and crispy. Remove to a plate lined with kitchen paper and discard the garlic.

Heat your widest pasta pan with a couple of tablespoons of oil and add the other garlic clove. Turn it over in the hot oil until golden on all sides and remove, turning down the heat.

Add the pasta to a pan of salted boiling water and at the same time break the nduja into the pan of garlic oil, warming it slowly to release its goodness: don't let it fry too much.

Add the marjoram leaves and drained pasta once almost cooked (reserve some of the cooking water) and toss with most of the breadcrumbs. Add the cooking liquid to loosen, letting the pasta soak up all the other flavours in the pan for 2 minutes.

Serve on a warmed platter with the rest of the breadcrumbs sprinkled over.

CHICKPEA GNOCCHI AND ROSEMARY

GNOCCHI DI CECI CON SALVIA

Like all gnocchi made with potato these are best cooked and eaten as quickly as possible. Mixing the potatoes with chickpeas is a more unusual combination, bringing an earthiness to the flavour of the gnocchi. These are, of course, also ace with tomato sauce.

FOR 3

100g dried chickpeas, soaked overnight in cold water

200g floury potatoes, scrubbed

100g '00' flour, plus extra for dusting

1 egg

nutmeg

1 lemon

1 garlic clove, sliced

1 good tbsp butter

1 rosemary sprig, leaves only

500ml whole milk

grated Parmesan (optional)

sea salt, black pepper and extra virgin olive oil

Drain the chickpeas and place in a large pan with plenty of fresh water (no salt!). Bring to the boil and cook until soft. This should take an hour so you can use the time to boil the potatoes in salted water until tender when pierced with a skewer, or the point of a knife. Drain and allow the potatoes to steam dry in the colander until they are cool enough to handle. Peel the skins off with your fingers or by scraping with a knife.

Once the chickpeas are tender, drain thoroughly and return to the hot pan to allow them to steam off the heat for a minute. Pass the potatoes and chickpeas together through a potato ricer or food mill (mouli). This takes a bit of effort and is much easier if the chickpeas are still warm.

Lay a cotton tea towel or napkin onto a board, sprinkle with flour and set aside.

Scatter half the flour onto the worktop and spread the potato and chickpea mash on top. Make a well and break in the egg, grate over a little nutmeg, and add the remaining flour.

With both your hands open like shovels, fold the mixture in on itself from the edges and then top and bottom. Keep moving it until you have a dough. It is a skill to bring the dough together without over-kneading but this helps keep the gnocchi light. It is possible that you will need a bit more flour if the dough seems too sticky. Don't add too much, though, or it will make the gnocchi rubbery.

Take a fist-sized piece of dough and, with a light touch, roll with your hands. Make a sausage about 2cm in diameter. Dust with flour and cut into 2cm chunks with a butter knife to form your gnocchi. Use the knife to shuffle them across the work surface as you go so they are further dusted in flour. Transfer them to the lined board, taking care that they don't touch each other, and set aside while you make the sauce.

To make the sauce, peel small pieces of rind from the lemon with a potato peeler.

Put the garlic into a wide pan with a tablespoon of olive oil and the butter. Season with salt and allow to fry a little. Add the rosemary and lemon peel. When the rosemary has turned a vivid green, add the milk and bring to the boil, then simmer to reduce. Add a tiny squeeze of lemon juice as you do so to help it curdle. Season with salt and pepper.

Cook the gnocchi in boiling salted water. When they have floated to the surface they are ready to scoop out and serve with the rosemary sauce, adding freshly grated Parmesan if you wish.

MIXED PASTA WITH JERUSALEM ARTICHOKES

PASTA MISTA AL TOPINAMBUR

The bags of *pasta mista* – literally mixed shapes of pasta – from grand pasta factories have become a favourite of mine. They work excellently with anything a bit soupy like this or *pasta e fagioli*. If you can't find any, break up long pasta and mix with the ends of other packets to replicate the real thing. This dish also works with cavatelli; just shorten the cooking time.

FOR 4

350g Jerusalem artichokes

1 onion, sliced

2 celery sticks, sliced

75g smoked pancetta, diced

3 tbsp tomato sauce, passata or Pommarola (page 100)

350g *pasta mista*

50g Parmesan, plus a small piece of rind

sea salt, black pepper and extra virgin olive oil

Peel and cube the Jerusalem artichokes, and leave them in fresh water to stop them oxidising. Put the onion, celery and pancetta in a large saucepan with 2 tablespoons of oil and a pinch of salt, and sweat over a medium heat. Cook for 10 minutes until the onion and celery are soft and translucent and some of the pancetta coloured and melted.

Add the tomato sauce and turn up the heat. Cook briskly to reduce the tomato – which will take a matter of minutes – and then add the drained artichokes and cheese rind. Cover with a litre of water and boil for about 5 minutes.

Then add the pasta with enough liquid to cover. When the liquid has returned to the boil, add a pinch of salt and cook, stirring from time to time. Add more water if needed.

When much of the water has evaporated or been absorbed, and the pasta is cooked, stir in the cheese. Taste and adjust the seasoning – a good grind of pepper is required. Serve right away.

COLD PIZZOCCHERI
PIZZOCCHERI FREDDI

This is what to make if, like me, you are someone who likes to watch Japanese soba masters making noodles on YouTube. This pasta is much rougher, but I like it anyhow. In Italy, pizzoccheri are almost always served in the traditional way, with cabbage, potatoes and alpine cheese. Here they are cool, fresh and light – perfect for a late summer lunch.

FOR 4

200g buckwheat flour
50g '00' flour
125ml water
⅛ garlic clove
300g ripe salad tomatoes, chopped
1 tbsp capers
½ bunch basil
250g potatoes, peeled and diced
50g Parmesan, grated
sea salt and extra virgin olive oil

To make the pizzocheri, mix the two flours together in a bowl and then add the water. Use your hands to combine everything as thoroughly as possible before moving the dough to a floured worktop and kneading for a few minutes. Despite having very little gluten, the dough will become smoother quite quickly. It's not necessary to knead excessively. Wrap in cling film and rest for an hour.

Meanwhile, crush the garlic with the back of a knife with a little salt. Squeeze out some of the juice from the tomatoes before mixing them with the garlic and a little more salt in a large salad bowl. Add the capers and basil, tearing the leaves into the bowl. Mix with 3 tablespoons of olive oil. Allow everything to stand for at least half an hour.

Once rested, roll out the pasta dough on a lightly floured worktop (do it in two batches if you like) until about 2mm thick. Cut into strips about 2cm across by 6cm long. Transfer to a floured board, tray or large plate as you do so.

Boil the potatoes in a large pan of salted water. After 5 minutes add the pasta and cook for 8 minutes. Drain before combining with the tomatoes and grated cheese.

SPAGHETTI WITH FRESH MACKEREL AND OLIVES

SPAGHETTI CON SGOMBRO E OLIVE

I had intended to include an updated tuna pasta here as another throwback to my student days, but this mackerel sauce won the day as it's so tasty. I urge you to try poached mackerel – it's quick, unusual and surprisingly delicate.

FOR 4

1 large fresh mackerel, gutted (by you or a kind fishmonger) and head discarded

2 bay leaves

1 garlic clove, sliced

50g butter

20 green olives, chopped

½ bunch rocket in winter or basil in summer, chopped

zest of 1 lemon, plus extra (optional)

1 tbsp capers

400g linguine, or other dried pasta of your choice

sea salt, black pepper (including some whole corns) and extra virgin olive oil

Put the fish, bay leaves, garlic (bar one slice), a few black peppercorns and salt in a pan and add cold water to just cover. Bring slowly to the boil over a medium heat. When it reaches boiling point, turn off the heat and leave the pan covered. After 8 minutes in the water the fish should be cooked, so when it is cool enough to handle, flake the meat from the bones, removing some skin as you do so.

Crush the remaining garlic slice with the back of a knife. Add to a bowl with the fish and the butter. Season well with pepper and mush together with a fork. Add the olives, rocket, lemon zest and capers with 2 tablespoons of olive oil to loosen and stir to combine. Taste, adding extra lemon zest if you like.

Cook the pasta in boiling salted water and use half a ladleful of the pasta water to slightly warm and loosen the sauce. Drain the pasta when al dente, reserving another cup of the cooking water, and toss with the sauce, judging whether or not you need any more liquid to get the sauce to the right creamy consistency.

You can adapt this recipe by serving with toasted golden breadcrumbs scattered on top, or indeed some grated cheese.

CAVATELLI WITH SALT COD AND CRUNCHY PEPPERS

CAVATELLI CON BACCALÀ E PEPERONI CRUSCHI

Omit the peppers by all means. I have used dried chillies before with good results but it's a bit of a lottery if you open a new pack. There's a knack to making the pasta but it's not impossible – and much easier than orecchiette, but you know you can buy both ready-made too.

FOR 4

100g semola flour, plus extra for dusting

200g pasta flour

100g spelt flour

200ml water

200g cauliflower, chopped

1 garlic clove, sliced

dried chilli, crumbled

250g salt cod, washed (see page 166)

40g pecorino (optional)

4 slices dried peppers (page 120; optional)

sea salt and extra virgin olive oil

Make a dough as described on page 25 but using the flours and water listed here, and rest for at least half an hour.

Cut a small walnut-sized – very roughly 50g – chunk of dough. Place on a large wooden board or directly on the work surface. Roll into a sausage just less than 1cm thick. Cut this into 4cm pieces so you have several little cylinders. That's the easy bit.

Place your three middle fingers on the top part of one cylinder, and press down and roll towards you at the same time. This should make a cavatello curled around your fingers which you can flick away to the back of your immediate work space before attempting the next. The centre will have been hollowed out but the edges should still be quite thick, and potentially nicely chewy. Dust them with a little flour to help prevent them sticking together and store them side by side, rather than on top of each other, on a tea towel-lined and floured board.

To make the sauce, boil the cauliflower in a pan of unsalted water. Fry the garlic in 2 tablespoons of oil in a separate wide pasta pan with a lid until golden. Then, working quickly so it doesn't burn, add flakes of chilli (I take the seeds out), the cod, skin side up, and a mug of water. Cover with the lid on and cook over a good heat for 10 minutes.

Remove the pan from the heat and the fish from the pan. Reserve the liquid. Scrape the skin off the cod with a knife. Flake half of the fish and place the other half in a mixer along with the cauliflower and some of the reserved liquid. Buzz and return to the pan along with the flaked cod. Mix gently.

Cook the pasta in boiling salted water for about 7 minutes or until they've been floating for a few minutes. Scoop out into the sauce, reserving some of the cooking water, and toss together. Add some pasta water should you need it, and cheese if you like – though I realise this is controversial – and crack over dried peppers if you have them.

PACCHERI WITH KALE AND WALNUTS

PACCHERI CON CAVOLO E NOCI

This has been a firm favourite at home for a good few years. Since I've been eating it, I have discovered that kale pesto is a (health) *thing*, but the recipes I have seen use lemon, which I can find challenging with pasta, and the kale is raw. Mine isn't too much less healthy and tastes really good.

FOR 4

1 slice sourdough bread
100ml organic whole milk
100g kale
½ garlic clove
80g Parmesan or pecorino, grated
50g walnuts, shelled
400g paccheri, or other short pasta
sea salt and extra virgin olive oil

Soak the bread in the milk. Bring a pan of salted water to the boil, add the kale and boil it for 5 minutes. Drain the kale (reserve all the water) and place in a food processor bowl along with the soaked bread (reserve the milk), garlic, cheese and walnuts. Blitz, then stir in 4 tablespoons of olive oil. Use a little of the reserved kale water and milk to thin the sauce to the desired consistency, and taste for salt.

Cook the pasta in the same water the kale was cooked in. This dish is nice if the pasta is really al dente – try it a good minute earlier than it says on the packet and, if it's cooked, drain (reserve a little of the cooking liquid) and mix with the sauce. This can be done quickly over a gentle heat adding a little reserved pasta water if needed.

SPAGHETTI WITH CLAMS COOKED LIKE RISOTTO

SPAGHETTI ALLE VONGOLE RISOTTATO

This is a classic pasta dish adapted to cook everything together in the same pan. The starchiness of the clam sauce will significantly raise your *Spaghetti alle Vongole* game.

FOR 2

500kg clams
1 garlic clove
1 dried chilli, plus extra (optional)
small bunch parsley
100ml dry white wine
200g spaghetti
knob of butter
sea salt and extra virgin olive oil

The best way to clean clams is to check each one individually. The shells should be closed with them still alive. Then rinse well before leaving in cold, salted water (a handful of salt will do it) for several hours, or overnight in the refrigerator. This purges the clams of any remaining sand. Rinse them again.

Put 2 tablespoons of oil, the garlic, chilli and some of the parsley sprigs in a pan set over a medium heat. When the garlic is golden, remove, add the clams, toss, and then quickly follow with the wine and cover.

Shuffle the pan from time to time with the lid on. When the clams are cooked and open, remove from the heat. Pick the clams from their shells, saving the juice.

Bring a pan of salted water to the boil and begin to cook the spaghetti as you would normally. At the same time, bring the clam liquid to the boil in a wide pan.

After cooking for 2 minutes, use tongs to transfer the spaghetti to the clam pan. Add 2 ladlefuls of the pasta water, and begin to cook, stirring. Keep stirring and simmering. The amount of time it will take varies between pasta brands, but it's probably 1 minute more than the time stated on the packet.

Once the first liquid has almost disappeared, you may need to add another ladleful of pasta cooking water. The trick is for the pasta to arrive al dente at the moment the sauce is dense and rich, so don't overdo it.

When satisfied, turn off the heat and add the clam meat, which you can chop if the clams are particularly large, plus the rest of the parsley, chopped, and the butter. Check the seasoning – I sometimes like a little extra flaked chilli.

PENNE AND PORCINI COOKED LIKE RISOTTO

PENNE PORCINI E ZAFFERANO

A late convert to cooking pasta like risotto, I love the way the starch in the pasta can thicken into a sauce. It is possible to add nothing more than oil. This is the pasta version of possibly my favourite risotto. The measurements for the size of pan and amount of water are just to get you started. They will vary depending on your pasta brand and, once you've got the feel of cooking pasta like this, please judge by eye.

FOR 2

2 garlic cloves

1 celery stick, cut into 1cm slices

10g dried porcini

1 parsley sprig

180g pennette

pinch saffron fronds

knob of butter (optional)

50g grated Parmesan

sea salt, black pepper and extra virgin olive oil

Bring 3 litres of water to the boil with the garlic cloves, celery, porcini and parsley, plus a pinch of salt. Allow to simmer until the garlic is very soft, about 10–15 minutes.

Add the pasta and saffron.

Simmer and keep stirring so the pasta cooks evenly. It should take a minute or two longer than it would normally. The idea is for almost all of the liquid to evaporate evenly as the pasta cooks. It is better to keep the pan on the dry side and turn the pasta over in order to cook uniformly than have it too wet. Add a ladleful of water from time to time if needed.

When thick and cooked add a drizzle of oil, or indeed a knob of butter if you'd rather, and the cheese and stir. Allow to sit for 3 minutes with a lid on before serving so that the sauce finishes thickening and soaks even more into the penne.

VEGETABLES
VERDURE

Grammi
1Kg 900 800 700 600 500 400 300 200 100 0
PISA
FTP

VEGETABLES

The reason to cook vegetables is because they are versatile. The reason to eat them is because they are exquisite. But vegetables are far more than just the backbone of the kitchen. A walk past your local greengrocer's or through the market is a window into the seasons. Knowing what is growing and when keeps you aware of the seasons, which is of particular benefit in the city, where you can feel otherwise disconnected from nature.

Like many modern cooks, my cooking practice is to go to the market first, and then decide what to eat from the ingredients on offer, rather than shop with a preconceived notion of what is for supper. This is how we write the menus at work too. It's more often the vegetables that set the tone: and not which vegetables, but at what stage they are at in their growth and tenderness. One of the finest examples of this is the broad bean, which can have a couple of seasons. When the bright green pods first appear in the spring, they are best podded as close as possible to the garden they were grown in and eaten raw. Following this stage, they need flash cooking, and their still tender leaves are also delicious in salad. As the months move on, the starchier beans require a bit more soaking and often double-podding, eventually splitting before they get too mealy to handle. If it is sunny enough and the pods are left on the plant to dry, they transform once more into a pulse with an incredible depth of flavour and versatility.

Shopping in season is second nature to me. The reasons for this are twofold. Vegetables, like a lot of things, are often at their cheapest when they are at their best and most plentiful, and I enjoy reaping the financial rewards – as well as the taste benefit – of eating in the moment. Yet vegetables have a short shelf life, shorter often than meat or fish. This might go some way to explaining why, in the two decades I have been cooking professionally, I have seen lots of greengrocers close down, while speciality butchers and even fishmongers have been on the rise. We seem more prepared to spend money on meat than on greens, and to feel greater concern about the adverse effects of eating 'bad' meat than consuming low-grade vegetables.

I hope the trend is changing. Vegetables have become hip – particularly wild, 'foraged' ones. Two new greengrocers have opened in my borough in the last couple of years and both are thriving. Then there are the amazing farmers' markets. What a lovely return to a traditional method of shopping. On a day off, a visit to a farmers' market has become a family ritual, quite as much as, if not more than, the Sunday papers, especially now that we have young kids. The whole family troops along, our daughter impatient for the playground but persuadable enough if we are quick.

I remember Giovanni Manetti, the famous wine-maker, saying that his first reason for farming organically was that his house and children live in the middle of the vineyards. I think that says it all. My family and I eat organic whenever possible, which today can be really quite often. That said, there are of course other ways to choose, and I tend to trust my palate first in these matters.

Back in Italy, we have discovered a new grower below our town who sells direct to the public. It's an extremely 'slow' shopping experience. You arrive in his shed to be met by the yapping of a small dog. Pietro, the grower, is most often nowhere to be seen, in the middle of some laborious task such as milling his own polenta. When you track him down, he changes into his boots and asks you what you're interested in – let's say leeks – and then how many you would like. You watch as he stomps over the land, through neat rows of plants growing at different stages, bending to pull one, two, three leeks, hacking off the fronds and greenest tips. He returns to you for his next instruction – say radicchio. Those red and white furled heads are added to the basket along with the carrots he'll rinse surplus earth from using his outdoor tap. Pietro takes special requests, like *cime* tops, but you pay more. He changes back into his clogs before weighing out the booty, which is so absurdly reasonable that you wonder how he can possibly make a living from his work. This is a nirvana for vegetable lovers and Pietro is my father's absolute hero.

I am deeply attached to my southern Italian food idyll, where vegetables take centre stage, but it's important to see it in context. If buying vegetables in season has cost incentives to us now, those were absolute imperatives to my grandmother. She survived on a genuinely frugal, largely vegetable-based diet. Perhaps because of this, she fervently appreciates any meat she tastes. This highlights that the predominance of vegetables to cooking in some regions of Italy was born from the necessities and urgencies of hunger and poverty. We are lucky enough to be better off today, and to be able to make choices about what we spend our money, be it animal or vegetable.

The recipes within this chapter constitute a true appreciation of all things plant-based. In central Italy, the ritual *pinzimonio* celebrates the pressing of the new oil: a table piled high with crisp fresh vegetables, usually celery, carrots, fennel bulbs and whole artichokes. There is something primeval about ripping through unprepared vegetables with your hands dripping in salt and oil. It is in this spirit that the recipes in this chapter have evolved.

They are often based much around the vegetables that land on the doorstep in our vegetable box scheme rather than imported from Italy. I like to apply the same touch to the Brussels sprouts, parsnips, turnips and even swedes at home that one struggles to find in the Italian garden.

The first few are preserves, or pretend preserves. I like to have some of these kicking about as they are great for extending time at the table. We eat them before or after our main food. Piquant excuses to pour another glass and linger longer together.

Afford vegetables time prior to cooking. A general rule is that slower cooking can involve less prep, while quick cooking is more labour intensive at the start. Enjoy this preparation and consider your vegetables before everything else. The best thing is the way they can be adapted to different cooking techniques and flavours. I can think of more ways to prepare an aubergine than a steak.

BOTTLED GREEN BEANS

FAGIOLINI SOTT'OLIO

I typically eat these cold with a piece of cheese, slice of bread and another vegetable, turning them into a whole course. Made with runner beans from the garden, cutting them into strips to fit the jar is a great way to use your crop up while it's in peak condition. It is possible to make with almost any vegetable: artichokes, cauliflower, carrots, courgettes or aubergines. It is, however, critical to guard against botulism when preserving by following these rules:

- **Wash your hands**
- **Clean the kitchen and utensils with detergent**
- **Preserve fruit and vegetables of high quality only**
- **Wash ingredients well; avoid any that are bruised**
- **Use stainless-steel saucepans**
- **Use glass jars and store in the dark**
- **Use the right amount of vinegar, lemon, salt or sugar**
- **Sterilise the jars**
- **Ensure the jars are properly sealed**

MAKES 2 X 500G JARS

300ml wine vinegar (any type)

700ml water

1kg green beans, topped, tailed and washed

8 garlic cloves

8 basil leaves

2 chillies

sea salt and extra virgin olive oil

Properly sterilise your cleaned jars by bringing them to the boil in a large pan of water. It is best to line the pan with a clean towel to stop them hitting each other. Once they have come to the boil, keep over the heat for 20 minutes, then turn off and let the jars cool down. Include the lids in the boiling. The best practice is to use new lids. Definitely discard any that look ropy.

Bring the vinegar to the boil in a medium pan with the water and a small fistful of salt. Add the beans and cook for 5 minutes. You can do this in batches. Drain and allow to dry completely, using a clean tea towel if you like.

Fill the jars halfway with the beans, and add 2 garlic cloves, 2 basil leaves and a chilli to each. Cover with olive oil and use the end of a spoon to wiggle the beans in as much as possible, paying attention not to trap air inside and allowing it instead to bubble out. Fill with the remaining beans, garlic and basil and top up with oil. Ensure that the

beans are a couple of centimetres from the top of the jar, that they are totally covered with olive oil, and move with the end of a knife to allow as much air to escape as possible.

Put the sterilised lids on the jars and return them to the pan of water using a towel to keep them in place so they don't bump into each other. Boil the jars for 30 minutes, before allowing to cool (either in the water or out of it).

Store in a cool, dark place for at least a month before opening. Once open, keep in the fridge and eat within a week. If there is any sign that the oil or beans have discoloured, are fizzy, or the button in the lid doesn't pop, discard the jars.

CLAAS

PRESERVING TOMATOES | CONSERVE DI POMODORO

I tried to have an allotment but failed. Maybe one day I'll be able to allocate the time necessary, but in the meantime, I content myself with growing only in my small London yard. We are self-sufficient in herbs, have a little salad and there are specific crops – courgettes, mostly for their flowers, broad beans and tomatoes – that we cultivate.

There is nothing more satisfying than opening the small jars of tomatoes in the cupboard that we have bottled during the summer months. An instant and delicious pasta sauce, they are also useful in adding body to other dishes. Jarring tomatoes takes a lot of effort so I tend to be mean with them and use them sparingly in conjunction with other things: some slow-cooked meat, to coat greens or flicked around eggs. There are lots of ways to preserve a small tomato crop but I have decided that these two are best for bringing out every ounce of flavour, which is important in the UK. For many years, I made do with rinsing the tomato juice from the tins of plum tomatoes I bought from the supermarket. Now I rely on these small, homemade jars and supplement them with expensive bottled tomatoes from the south of Italy that don't contain preservatives other than salt. I have on several occasions found a day in the summer to get together with friends and make lots of jars of tomatoes bought when they are at their best and cheapest. Nothing makes me feel more like an Italian immigrant.

TOMATO SAUCE
LA POMMAROLA

You can buy a red plastic dedicated tomato mill for not much. This will pass the tomatoes as it removes the skins. A regular food mill (mouli) will do the same and a lot more besides – a worthwhile investment. Otherwise it is better to peel them first. Scoring, quickly boiling and then plunging in iced water will facilitate this.

MAKES 20 X 500ML JARS

15kg tomatoes

½ onion, thinly sliced

20 basil leaves

sea salt and extra virgin olive oil

EQUIPMENT

large cooking pot

food mill

funnel

sterilised jars (see page 94) – I use the smallest jam jars I can find so that I never have leftovers; use new lids each year, it's worth it

tea towels

Clean the tomatoes really well. Remove any blemishes and cut them in half, removing the eye where the stalk attaches as you do so. Put them in a large pot and bring to the boil. Boil for half an hour, until they look very soft. They will probably release a lot of water, depending on the type of tomato you have grown or bought. You can cook this down rather than pour it away as it is all flavour.

Pass the tomatoes through the mill while still hot, turning them to pulp and removing the skins. Some people choose to pass the skins twice to get everything out of them, but I rarely bother.

Heat a small amount of olive oil in the cooking pot and sweat the onion with some salt. Add the tomatoes after 5 minutes or so and continue to cook, simmering, uncovered, for at least 1½ hours. This slow cooking is essential for bringing out the flavour. It is not something that can be rushed; consider it an investment in future time-saving. Stir regularly and keep the temperature low enough to avoid it catching. Taste, and add more salt if it needs it. Salt is essential to preserving but be careful, as further cooking will concentrate the saltiness. There is no formula for the right amount.

Remove the tomatoes from the stove when you have a dense sauce, but not so dense that it is thick or jammy. Using a wide funnel, fill your sterilised jars to the top, keeping the rim clean. Slip an impeccably clean, unbruised basil leaf into each, being careful not to introduce air with it. I avoid adding garlic, chilli or pepper, but I always add a basil leaf when I bottle for the joy of the smell as I open the jar. There is no harm in adding a teaspoon of olive oil on top of the tomatoes as well, for extra security.

Screw the lids on, as tightly as you can, while the jars are still hot. You will need to use a cloth to tighten them fully. Place the jars lid down in several large pots and cover with tea towels to stop them moving around. Fill with water and boil for 40–60 minutes. Then let them cool down in the water overnight. It's hard work and, if you're like me, you'll be finishing in the small hours, but it's amazing to come down in the morning and see your jars all ready for storing. Store in a cool, dark place, keeping them in the fridge for a couple of days once opened.

If the lid should blow and the tomato fizzes, please don't use it! But if you follow the method carefully, particularly the last boiling, this will not be an issue.

JARRED TOMATOES
POMODORO IN VASETTI

Make a jar or two of these if you have exceptional tomatoes on your hands. Done correctly, this method will preserve their freshness well. Smash them into toast in the place of fresh tomatoes.

MAKES 1 X 1KG JAR

roughly 1.5kg tomatoes, not squishy (under-ripe is fine)

4 oregano or basil sprigs

1 garlic clove, sliced

black peppercorns

red wine vinegar

sea salt and extra virgin olive oil

Sterilise your jar (see page 94).

Carefully wash and dry the tomatoes, and cut them in half. If you have cherry tomatoes, use as they are; if plum tomatoes, scoop out the centres using a teaspoon. Make the first layer of tomatoes at the bottom of the jar. Place a sliver of garlic on top, some oregano leaves, a few peppercorns and sprinkle with salt and a little vinegar. Pour in a little oil before adding the next layer of tomatoes and repeating the process.

Once the jar is full, finish with a layer of oil so that no air gets in. Tap the jar with a spoon to release any trapped bubbles. Screw on the lid and place in a large pot of water. Once boiling, turn down the heat and simmer for 40 minutes. Turn off and allow to cool completely in the water before drying and storing somewhere cool and dark. Try to avoid keeping them out on display, despite how pretty they are. Once opened, store in the fridge and eat within a few days.

RED PEPPERS IN VINEGAR

PEPERONI SOTT'ACETO

A couple of times a year, Nonna used to put chillies under vinegar to use as a condiment. They are a distinctive flavour of the south of Italy. In Bisaccia, they have several varieties of spicy chillies well suited to this recipe. However, they are impossible to come by elsewhere, so a way to work around this is by using sweet peppers with some hot chilli. And, if we are cheating anyway, why not go the whole hog and boil them so that they can be used right away? Thus I have included two modes of preparation, a fast and a slow.

MAKES 2 X 500G JARS

1 litre white wine vinegar

200ml water

1kg hot round red peppers or sweet chillies, washed

8 garlic cloves, halved

20g sea salt

handful of fresh oregano, leaves picked and stalks reserved

THE SLOW WAY

Sterilise the jars (see page 94).

Bring the vinegar to the boil with the water and salt. Add the peppers and garlic. Boil for 4 minutes, turning the peppers once they bob to the surface.

Remove the peppers and transfer to the jars, reserving the vinegar. Include the garlic and add the oregano leaves. Pack in with the end of a wooden spoon so there is as little space as possible between them.

Fill with the vinegar while it's still hot. Make sure the peppers are below the level of the vinegar. Bend the oregano stalks and fit them into the lids; this helps to keep the peppers under the vinegar. Use a tea towel to close the lids tightly. Invert the jars until completely cold.

Store in a cool, dark place and don't open for at least a month. They will keep well if below the vinegar level at all times. Refrigerate once opened.

MAKES 2 X 500G JARS

1kg sweet red peppers, washed

1 hot red chilli, halved

200ml vinegar

600ml water

5 garlic cloves

15g sea salt

THE IMPATIENT WAY

Pierce the peppers here and there with a knife. Put everything into a medium pan, cover with a lid, and boil for 30 minutes. Turn over at least once during the cooking. There will be relatively little liquid left. Turn off and allow to cool completely.

They'll last a while covered in the fridge but the idea is to use them quickly.

PADRÓN PEPPERS AND MUSHROOMS

PEPERONI VERDI E FUNGHI

I continue to enjoy the flavour of strong vegetables cooked in tandem with different peppers, making use of their slight heat. Here are Padrón peppers because you can easily find them nowadays and they have an interesting flavour. Shiitake mushrooms are also easy to find and their dense nature makes them stand up well to poaching; an underrated way of cooking mushrooms that I learnt about in Liguria. Another example of super-simple cooking producing flavoursome results. Much better cold, don't be tempted to eat these while still warm.

FOR 4

3 garlic cloves

2 bay leaves

1 tsp black peppercorns

50ml good-quality vinegar

250g Padrón peppers, destalked and deseeded

400g shiitake mushrooms and/or girolles, oyster or a meaty variety, washed

extra virgin olive oil

In a large pan bring about a litre of water to the boil with the garlic, bay leaves, peppercorns and vinegar. Allow the garlic to soften for 8 minutes.

Add the peppers and mushrooms and boil for 10 minutes. The peppers will bob to the surface so cover with a lid to help them cook.

Drain well and let them steam dry for a couple of minutes. Dress with plenty of olive oil and allow to cool completely to room temperature. Eat them on their own as an antipasto or with fresh cheese to make a bigger course.

STUFFED AND ROASTED CHILLIES

PEPERONCINI AL FORNO

Choose your chillies well and you can eat them whole. I like to eat these with some fresh cheese that counteracts their heat. A great way to stir up an appetite and a thirst.

FOR 4

8 olives, pitted and chopped

20g capers

150g breadcrumbs

zest of 1 lemon

1 tbsp dried oregano

1 egg

8 large fresh long chillies, halved lengthways and deseeded

sea salt and extra virgin olive oil

Preheat the oven to 180°C/fan 160°C/gas 4.

Mix the olives with the capers, breadcrumbs, lemon zest and oregano in a small bowl. Season with salt before adding the egg and a tablespoon of oil and mixing everything together.

Stuff the chillies with the olive mixture. Set them on a baking tray with another glug of oil. Cover with foil and roast for 20 minutes or until soft. Allow to cool before eating.

EXTRA VIRGIN OLIVE OIL | OLIO EXTRAVERGINE DI OLIVA

In the summer of 1986, I found myself in Tuscany replanting an olive grove that had been killed by an exceptionally harsh winter. A lazy urban English kid, I found the labour surprisingly rewarding. On the hill's edge I remember having my first taste of proper grassy-peppery olive oil from the year before. It blew my socks off. I had no idea oil could taste so good. This was a formative foodie experience for me, by which I mean the discovery of something new, better than the norm. It was about as different from the bottles you could buy in the supermarket then as a just-picked strawberry is to one packaged up in midwinter. Once you know how good olive oil can taste there is no looking back. Later, as a chef, I found myself within a mile of the property where I had replanted the trees, buying oil with Ruthie and Rose. A team of us go back every year to taste the first of the new season oil, which opens the eyes of new chefs as it once did me.

This is no health book and I am not going to harp on about the claims surrounding olive oil. That it helps guard against various cancers, reduces the risk of type 2 diabetes, Alzheimer's, protects against depression, fights osteoporosis, helps the heart and may prevent strokes I am no expert on. What I can say for sure is that the astringent, delicious, fruity flavour of olive oil stimulates and coats the mouth in a way to make food – in my opinion, any food – taste better. It's a basic seasoning in my life and in my kitchen.

Thus almost all of the recipes throughout the book call for olive oil – and garlic. You can always leave the garlic out if you wish but never the oil. The type of cooking that is in this book would be as inauthentic without it as stir-frying without a wok. Olive oil is the cornerstone of Italian cooking.

My father asserts that the cliché is true: when he moved from Florence to Sheffield in 1970, it was only possible to find olive oil in a vial at the pharmacy. It could be argued that the battle for olive oil in Britain has been well won. Over the decades since my father moved over here, there has been more interest than ever in the healthful benefits of a Mediterranean way of eating. The diets of the Portuguese, Spanish and Greeks, as well as the southern Italians, rich in pulses, grains and vegetables, were held up for emulation.

And then there was the elixir, olive oil. Now we in England are the sixth largest olive oil consumer. It's already in over 50 per cent of homes and I reckon all of yours.

'Extra virgin olive oil' simply means that the olives have had their juice extracted mechanically without any additives, chemical or otherwise, at a low temperature. In recent years, ever more producers have begun picking olives earlier in the season – some time between October and November – when their flavour is at its peak. Better growers press their olives within hours of picking rather than days, in clean modern mills that press less per kilo than before. Filtering (removing solids in the oil) is still controversial among the elite producers. It does help preserve quality over time. Ideally you would use unfiltered oil at the start of the season and move onto lightly filtered oil after three months.

Sadly the popularity and increased demand for olive oil seems to have led to a level of unscrupulousness on the part of some producers and companies. Unclean practices have been highlighted in the press. Clever packaging obfuscates the origin and quality of the olives. Here are some guidelines for buying oil:

- Make sure it is in a dark bottle or container. It is unlikely that someone producing the best oil would allow it to spoil in contact with the light
- Buy oil with two years hence best before date, confirming that's it's from the current harvest
- Look for oil that is estate produced and preferably bottled
- Pay as much as you can afford. If Extra virgin olive oil cost as much as a pair of handmade shoes 60 years ago, one can't expect a £5.99 litre of oil to be up to much today
- See if the variety or varieties of olives in the bottle are named
- Get to know a couple that you like and return to them. See how different years compare

We only ever have extra virgin oil at home and always in at least two qualities. Simplistically, there is one olive oil for cooking and another for finishing, the former softer, fruitier and rounder and the latter more astringent and expensive.

PARSNIPS UNDER OIL
PASTINACHE SOTT'OLIO

I've never eaten parsnips in Italy but I regularly find myself trying to use them up when they arrive here. This instant sott'olio is especially good with salami. Choose a good-quality vinegar you particularly like; maybe not balsamic but any other. The vinegar goes really well set against the sweetness of the parsnips. You will need a large serving dish that will accommodate the parsnips one or two slices deep.

FOR 6

2 tbsp pine nuts

1 tbsp coriander seeds

1 tbsp black peppercorns

1kg parsnips, scrubbed and cut into 1cm chunks

2 garlic cloves, finely sliced

1 tbsp finely chopped marjoram leaves and/or rosemary and/or parsley

best-quality vinegar

sea salt and extra virgin olive oil

Preheat the oven to 150°C/fan 130°C/gas 2. Spread the pine nuts out on a baking tray and roast for 15–20 minutes tossed in a teeny amount of oil with a pinch of salt. Keep an eye on them as they could be ready before. They should be a lovely pale gold colour rather than mahogany.

Bring a pan of salted water to the boil with the spices. Add the parsnips in batches – each batch will require just 4 minutes once the water returns to the boil. Remove to the serving dish with a slotted spoon and dress while warm with a generous 3–4 tablespoons of vinegar. On the last batch, sieve out the spices and spread over the parsnips.

Season with salt, layer with the sliced garlic and herbs and then drench with olive oil and pine nuts and allow to cool completely.

You can eat these at once but they are perhaps best the next day. They'll keep for a week in the fridge, covered.

AUBERGINES UNDER OIL

MELANZANE SOTT'OLIO

This really clogs up your fridge, but I promise it's worth it. Don't be concerned by the colour of the aubergines. They will discolour but eventually look great once fully marinated. These are best forgotten about at the back of the cupboard as they make a lovely discovery during the winter months. They take on a flavour and texture more like mushrooms, really interesting and a far cry from the ubiquitous grilled aubergine under oil you'll see in Italian delis. Make sure to work impeccably cleanly when preserving and sterilise your jars and lids before using (see page 94). Beware of fizzy preserves.

MAKES 2 X 500G JARS

1.5kg aubergines, preferably the pale Violetta type, washed and peeled

250ml wine vinegar (any type)

2 garlic cloves, finely chopped

1 celery heart with the leaves, finely chopped

½ bunch mint or herb of your choosing

1 red chilli, finely chopped

rosemary sprigs, or any woody herb

sea salt and extra virgin olive oil

Cut the aubergines into slices about 1.5cm thick and then across to make chips. Place in a plastic or other non-reactive bowl with two cups of water and a small fistful of salt. Leave them somewhere cool for a couple of hours before draining them into a colander – but don't rinse. Instead, return a handful to the original bowl, cover with a good sprinkling of salt, another layer of aubergines, another of salt and so on, until they're all used up. Be sure to finish with salt. Put a plate on them and place a heavy weight on top – the idea is to push out as much vegetable juice as possible.

Make space in the fridge and leave them weighted down so they are under the level of the brine they'll produce. Keep them like this for 6 days. On day 7, drain and rinse the aubergine chips in a sink of cold, clean water, then repeat. Give them a squeeze to remove any excess water and soak them in the vinegar for 30 minutes in a clean bowl.

Drain the aubergines and squeeze firmly rolled up inside at least one clean tea towel, wringing them out over the sink. Toss with the garlic, celery, herbs and chilli and fill up your sterilised jars.

Top up with olive oil. Bang the jars lightly on the worktop and move the contents around with a thin knife or skewer to burst any air pockets. Make sure that the level of the oil is above that of the aubergines. Use some washed rosemary or other woody herb sprigs to help them stay down in the jar. Screw on the lids and store somewhere cool and dark for at least 2 weeks.

Eat within a couple of months. Once open, store in the fridge.

FRIED AUBERGINES WITH MINT

MELANZANE ALLA SCAPECE

Alla scapece is an extension of the escabeche method of cooking in vinegar popular in all Latin countries. It is possible to omit the salting by using Violetta aubergines, but I think the more common variety have a texture better suited to this recipe. If you fry the aubergines correctly – putting them in only once the oil is hot – they should not be greasy. It is important to have kitchen paper ready to drain them on once they have been fried.

This recipe makes enough for four – as I say – but I often make a double batch as they last and are very moreish. I like to eat these with bread, as I do most things. They are good by themselves or alongside other cold vegetables, meats or cured fish.

FOR 4

2 aubergines

2 garlic cloves, peeled and roughly chopped

½ litre sunflower oil

2 red chillies

250ml wine vinegar (any type)

sea salt and extra virgin olive oil

Peel the aubergines, leaving four strips of skin on. Cut into rounds about 1cm thick. Place them in a colander, salting well between the layers. Leave a plate on top to help press out all the bitter juices. This will take roughly an hour.

Wash and dry the aubergines well before you heat the sunflower oil. I find it best to use a big wok to fry the aubergines. If you don't have one, use a pan with sides higher by three times the volume of oil. Test that the oil is hot by dropping in an end slice. If the oil is of a sufficiently high temperature it will immediately start to sizzle. Then carefully drop in the first round of aubergines – fry only a few at a time. Have a plate with kitchen paper ready to drain them on. After 2 minutes, once they are golden underneath, turn them over using tongs. Then remove them 2 minutes after that and do the same with the next batch.

When all the aubergines are cooked, fry the garlic in another pan with 2 tablespoons of olive oil. Add the chillies, which you can break apart a bit with your fingers to release the seeds, and then all the vinegar. Bring to the boil and then remove from the heat.

Place the aubergines in a ceramic dish and pour over the hot vinegar. Move them around so that they are all coated and look good.

You can enjoy these once they have cooled. Sealed in a clean container, they will keep excellently for up to a week in the fridge.

BARELY COOKED PUMPKIN

ZUCCA APPENA COTTA

This is best with a sweet pumpkin, importantly one that is absolutely ripe. The aim is to make the pumpkin al dente, not soft – just take the edge off it. It will therefore taste different from your usual roast pumpkin. I enjoy these with roasted whole hot chillies and sweet baked ricotta, a reminder of late summers in the south of Italy.

FOR 2

250g slice pumpkin, peeled and deseeded

¼ garlic clove, crushed

juice of ½ lemon

pinch dried oregano

sea salt, black pepper and extra virgin olive oil

Cut the pumpkin flesh into odd shapes a few mm thick, or perfect shapes depending on your character.

Bring a large pan of water to the boil and season well with salt. When the water reaches a rolling boil, add the pumpkin in small batches for 30 seconds, not longer. Remove, draining with a slotted spoon to a bowl. Add the garlic and lemon juice to the hot pumpkin, along with a pinch of salt, two cracks of black pepper, a good pinch of oregano and a slug of olive oil.

Leave to cool before eating but don't refrigerate.

SALTED COURGETTES

ZUCCHINI SALATI

The idea for this came from a delicious Szechuan salad where beansprouts are crushed after boiling and left to cool down in vinegar and chilli. This treatment is also nice with green beans but here courgettes are left raw, which makes an especially enjoyable texture of slice against slice.

FOR 4

400g courgettes

1 tbsp fresh oregano or mint or basil

3 tbsp good-quality wine vinegar

sea salt, black pepper or dried red chilli flakes and extra virgin olive oil

Slice the courgettes as thinly as possible, anyway you like. You could use a mandolin. Salt liberally and leave to drain in a colander over a plate.

After 30 minutes, once lots of vegetable juice has been released and when the slices look softer, give them a good rinse. Squeeze bone dry with your hands and dress with the herbs, vinegar, 3 tablespoons of olive oil and pepper or chilli.

Eat this as a first course at the start of a longer meal.

DRIED PEPPERS

PEPERONI SECCHI

Another way of preserving peppers is to dry them. I don't have a dehumidifier but I find that it works well in a regular fan oven if you open it from time to time to let the steam out. The oven method also replicates the flavour of a variety of long pepper that in southern Italy gets dried not for its heat but for a gentler aromatic quality. I bring strings of them home with me from holidays but they soon run out.

Only make this with fully ripe peppers at the height of the season. Add garlic, herbs, chilli and spices if you like, but I let the peppers do the talking and add other flavours when I use them in subsequent cooking, although you will get such a deep, rich and complex flavour that very few other ingredients are needed.

The peppers will take anywhere between 7 and 10 hours to dry depending on their thickness, the oven temperature and humidity. It is best to do this during a quiet day at home so you can check regularly. Gradually, all the rooms will fill with their aroma.

MAKES 2 BIG JARS

2kg red peppers, as thin-skinned as possible

¼ garlic clove, very finely chopped

sea salt, black pepper and extra virgin olive oil

Pre-heat the oven to 120°C/100°C fan/ gas mark ¼

Wash, dry and then slice the peppers into generous-sized pieces (they will shrink a lot). Clean them of seeds and remove the white pith should there be any.

Place them side by side, not overlapping, straight onto the baking racks of your oven.

After 30 minutes, open the oven door to allow the steam to escape. Repeat this for the first 3 hours, after which drop to hour-long intervals.

When they come out of the oven, dress with salt, pepper, a little raw garlic and olive oil.

They can be eaten like this on their own or as antipasti with several other dishes. But the reason to make them is to fry them and use to dress pasta, vegetables – typically potatoes – or fish.

CHRISTMAS SALAD

INSALATA NATALIZIA

There is an orange salad in every Italian cookbook and so it would be wrong to leave this out. I had heard from the Italian branch of my family about a celebratory sort of orange salad once eaten at Christmas with anchovies and *vino cotto* – which is cooked grape must. I was really excited about trying it when I was there one year, but I found it too sweet. This is a modified version of the one they used to have. It's also a good way to use your own cured sardines (see page 38) or if you have preserved herrings, which I find easily in my local Polish deli.

FOR 2

2 oranges

4 salted sardines, herrings or 6 anchovies

2 extra-thin slices lemon, chopped

½ sweet onion, thinly sliced

1 tsp red wine vinegar

2 tbsp black olives

1 teaspoon fennel seeds

fennel fronds, roughly chopped

sea salt, black pepper and extra virgin olive oil

Top and tail the oranges, and remove the skins without being too precious about leaving on a bit of the pith. Squeeze the tops and any scraggy pieces through your fingers into a bowl. Slice the oranges into neat pieces and arrange on your serving plate. Clean the fish if salty and cut into several pieces. Arrange on top of the oranges along with the lemon pieces and onion.

Add the vinegar, olives, fennel seeds and fronds to the bowl with the orange juice. Season and whisk in 2–3 tablespoons of oil and use to dress the salad.

WHITE BEAN CAKE
SFORMATO DI FAGIOLI

It takes just a few minutes to conjure up something that is as luxurious as it is earthy. Makes a great light meal paired with a green salad and a glass of wine, just as you might do with an omelette. Use beans you have soaked overnight and cooked yourself, or canned.

FOR 2

200g chicory, cavolo nero or another bitter green, roughly chopped

small bunch parsley

300g cannellini or other white beans soaked overnight and cooked

100ml double cream

50g provola or scamorza, coarsely grated

3 eggs

sea salt, black pepper and butter for greasing

Preheat the oven to 200°C/fan 180°C/gas 6.

Heavily butter a medium ovenproof dish, or a cake tin lined with baking paper, scrunched to help it fit.

Cook the chopped greens in boiling water for 7 minutes. Pick in the parsley leaves then immediately drain. When cool enough to handle, squeeze a little to remove excess water.

Blitz the beans in a food processor along with a ladleful of bean water. If using a tin of beans slightly warm them first. Add the cream, grated cheese, eggs, a nice pinch of salt and pepper and blitz again. It is okay to let the machine run a bit. Taste for seasoning.

Fill the dish or tin, scatter the greens over and drizzle with a little olive oil. Bake for 30 minutes. It will become golden and puff up a little. Eat while still warm.

VELVETY LEEKS
VELLUTATA

I like white sauce and think fondly of the penne with béchamel I used to have at university in Naples. It is a shame that is has become unfashionable to make sauces with flour but I find that if you use a good one you feel less bad about it.

Cooking like this really brings out the central ingredient, leeks in this case. Other vegetables also work well: potato and well-peeled celery together in equal quantities, or fennel – so use whatever tastes good that you have to hand.

Not really a soup but eat as such by itself or with a small piece of salty fish or meat. You can decide how thick you'd like it depending on what it accompanies.

FOR 2

400ml milk

2 cloves, chopped

4 bay leaves

nutmeg

2 garlic cloves, chopped

500g leeks, washed and sliced, including a lot of the darker tops

6 salted anchovy fillets

25g chickpea flour or wheat flour

small bunch parsley, chopped

sea salt, black pepper and extra virgin olive oil

Heat the milk with the cloves, bay leaves and a scratch of nutmeg in a small pan then allow to infuse for 30 minutes.

Fry the garlic in a medium pan with 3 tablespoons of olive oil. Before it starts to colour, add the leeks and cook for 5 minutes. Add the anchovies and flour at the same time. Stir constantly for 5 minutes over a medium heat. It'll get quite claggy – use two spoons to scrape all the flour off the base of the pan.

Add the infused milk in a stream, stirring all the while. It's much easier than you think to prevent lumps forming if you cook over a low heat, stirring often for 15 minutes. Add the parsley, season and cook for 3 minutes more, then blitz or blend.

If you'd rather it was thinner, add a little warm water before serving. It is also possible to add a couple of eggs to this and bake it in a well-buttered tin.

CABBAGE STUFFED WITH RICE

CAVOLO RIPIENO DI RISO

This is one of many alpine-inspired comfort dishes that help me to use up the endless supply of cabbages we receive in our veg box and warm us in the dark, cold months.

FOR 4

120g white short-grain or risotto rice

3 garlic cloves

150ml water

250ml whole milk

nutmeg

250g good-quality canned or jarred plum tomatoes, or Pommarola (page 100)

12 Savoy cabbage leaves

100g taleggio, diced

a few mint leaves

sea salt, black pepper and extra virgin olive oil

Boil the rice with 2 of the garlic cloves in the water and milk in a medium pan. When just cooked, roughly 8 minutes (you want a little bite), the liquid should have reduced substantially. Season with salt, pepper and a scratching of nutmeg and set aside to cool.

Drain and chop the tomatoes if using canned or jarred. Slice the remaining garlic clove and fry in 2 tablespoons of oil with a pinch of salt in a small pan. When just turning golden add the tomatoes, turn the heat down and allow to cook slowly, stirring, for 30 minutes.

Bring a pan of salted water to the boil and cook the cabbage leaves for 4 minutes. Set aside to drain. When cool, cut out the thickest of the central ribs and discard. If they seem very cooked plunge them into cold water, otherwise don't bother.

Preheat the oven to 200°C/fan 180°C/gas 6.

Stir the taleggio through the cooled rice. Divide and roll this mixture into 12 walnut-sized pieces. Place each one in the middle of a cabbage leaf and fold around the rice so no part of it is exposed. Place with the prettiest side facing up in a well-oiled heavy-based ovenproof dish. Cover with the tomatoes but do not overdo it. Drizzle with oil, grind over some pepper and loosely cover with baking paper. Bake for 30 minutes. Serve with the mint torn over for lift.

STUFFED SMALL PEPPERS

PEPERONI RIPIENI

I was sent a bag of small, mixed peppers in my vegetable box. My first instinct was to stuff them, like the beautiful jars of tuna-filled peppers one can buy. These are not the traditional method and are intended to be eaten straight away

FOR 4

500g medium potatoes, scrubbed

1 garlic clove

250g mixed small peppers

red wine vinegar

250g best-quality canned or jarred tuna

1 lemon

1 tbsp salted capers, rinsed

50g olives

small bunch basil

sea salt, black pepper and extra virgin olive oil

Preheat the oven to 190°C/fan 170°C/gas 5.

Boil the potatoes in salted water with the garlic until soft when pierced with a knife. Meanwhile, remove the tops of the peppers and scoop out the seeds. Place on a baking tray lined with baking paper, sprinkle with a little oil and vinegar, salt and pepper and roast until soft and sweet, about 20 minutes.

Peel the boiled potatoes and put through a potato ricer or mash well.

Empty the tuna into a bowl and mash in 2 tablespoons of olive oil with a fork. Grate over the zest of the lemon, squeeze in half of the lemon's juice and then mix with the potato, capers and olives. Tear in the basil.

When the peppers are cool enough to handle, stuff each with the tuna filling and allow the flavours to mingle for at least 30 minutes before eating.

CELERIAC, CELERY AND CHESTNUTS

SEDANO RAPA, SEDANO E CASTAGNE

I like to eat this with English gammon, but without makes a great vegetarian option. It was my friend Pete who first cooked me a whole celeriac and it was memorable. He carefully cleaned every little tendril root but, despite my best efforts, when I tried to do the same mine was still gritty so I chop them off. This method of cooking in milk with lemon to curdle it is borrowed from the classic Italian way of cooking lamb, chicken and pork.

FOR 4

12 large chestnuts

1 celeriac, washed with muddy roots trimmed (don't peel it)

4 garlic cloves

1 tsp fennel seeds

4 celery sticks, halved

200g piece of gammon, quartered

a few bay leaves

1 lemon, pared

300ml milk

sea salt, black pepper and extra virgin olive oil

Score the chestnuts and plunge them into boiling water for 5 minutes before skinning (or microwave on high for 3 minutes).

Heat some olive oil in a heavy-based pan just big enough to contain all the ingredients. Season the celeriac and begin to brown in the oil, turning until it is lightly coloured all over. If it doesn't fit in the pan simply cut it in half – it changes nothing.

Add the garlic and fry for a minute, followed by the fennel seeds and chestnuts. Then add the celery, gammon, bay leaves and lemon peel. Add the milk and boil for 5 minutes. Crumple up a piece of baking paper then unfold it and place loosely over the celeriac. Put a regular lid on too and turn the heat down to medium-low. Cook for 45 minutes, basting the celeriac with the liquid in the pot from time to time.

Remove the celeriac to a board and carve. If the sauce in the pot is thin, let it cook and reduce until you're happy. When it's ready, spoon all the good bits over the celeriac.

POTATOES COOKED IN TOMATO

PATATE IN UMIDO

Cooking 'in humidity', or stewing, is a great way to lock in integrity and flavour. It can be employed for a piece of sinewy meat or tough cuttlefish but also a vegetable. The following recipe is illustrative of this. It is one of the simplest imaginable, but adding any extras would be a shame. I'd eat this mid-summer with a piece of poached white fish and a pile of just-picked herbs. Or add an egg each towards the very end of cooking for a complete late-night snack.

FOR 4

5 garlic cloves

500g medium potatoes, such as Nicola or Désirée (avoid fluffy varieties), scrubbed, dried and cut into 1–2cm chunks

5 fresh or jarred cooking tomatoes, halved, or Pommarola (page 100)

4 eggs (optional)

sea salt, black pepper and extra virgin olive oil

Put a generous 3 tablespoons of olive oil and the garlic cloves in a heavy-based pan over a medium heat. When the garlic begins to smell inviting and the oil is hot, add the potatoes. Allow them to absorb the garlic-flavoured oil for a minute before adding the tomatoes and seasoning with salt and pepper.

Cover with baking paper and a lid and cook over a medium heat for about 20 minutes, checking from time to time. You can add a little water if it looks like the potatoes are sticking. If you want to add eggs, do so just as the potatoes are becoming completely tender.

ARTICHOKES, TOMATO AND CAPERS

CARCIOFI IN UMIDO

Another vegetable stewed in tomato, this is as good cold as it is hot. It can be used to dress pasta or rice, eaten with a hunk of bread or as a side to something else. I enjoy cooking it with red or white wine.

FOR 4

8 medium artichokes

½ lemon

1 garlic clove, sliced

1 rosemary sprig, leaves only

1 tbsp salted capers, rinsed

5 fresh or jarred cooking tomatoes, or 250g good-quality passata or Pommarola (page 100)

250ml wine

sea salt, black pepper and extra virgin olive oil

To clean the artichokes, first remove the tough outer leaves, snapping them down. Then trim around the base and stem, being aware that this is the prized part and cutting the stalk to a few centimetres. Then trim away the point of the artichokes and darkest parts of the green leaves.

Rotate the artichokes on the worktop upside down and press to open the leaves a bit, then continue to stretch them out with your fingers. Use a teaspoon to scoop out the choke, if any. Rub with the cut side of the lemon to stop them discolouring.

Tuck the garlic slivers and rosemary in between the artichoke leaves. Season well before turning them over in a small pan with 2 tablespoons of olive oil. Add the capers and cook for 2 minutes over a medium heat before adding the tomatoes and half of the wine. Cover with baking paper and a lid and turn the heat down so the artichokes can steam. It should take about 20 minutes. Slowly add the rest of the wine and a little water if needed during this time.

JERUSALEM ARTICHOKES WITH FENNEL AND PEAS

TOPINAMBUR E FINOCCHIO CON PISELLI

This is something for the winter when you need inspiration. Frozen peas give a welcome bit of green and the fennel adds some spice. I have never made this with fresh peas, but you can do if you like.

FOR 4

500g Jerusalem artichokes

2 fennel bulbs, trimmed

½ red onion, sliced

2 garlic cloves, sliced

500g frozen peas

10 mint leaves

2 parsley sprigs

1 lemon

sea salt, black pepper and extra virgin olive oil

Peel the Jerusalem artichokes and cut into wedges. Keep under water to stop them discolouring. Remove any stringy-looking outer parts of the fennel and cut into wedges 2cm thick.

Heat a heavy-based pan with 2 tablespoons of olive oil and sweat the onion with a pinch of salt, adding the garlic once the onion has softened. After 5 minutes, add the fennel and stew with a lid on for another 5 minutes.

Now add the Jerusalem artichokes with the peas and continue to stew for another 10 minutes over a low heat.

Jerusalem artichokes often cook unevenly, so pierce a chunk to see what you think. Check the seasoning and stir through the herbs with a little extra olive oil.

Serve with wedges of lemon to squeeze over.

CHARRED NEW POTATOES AND ARTICHOKES

CARCIOFI E PATATE ALLA BRACE

This is a recipe for the barbecue. There is another great dish called *carciofi arrostiti*: artichokes are stuffed with garlic, parsley and sometimes lardo and grilled, with the outsides blackened in the embers of a fire. I recommend anyone to try it given the opportunity, but it's annoying as you have to wait for the coals to die down and it makes your fingers black. This is something inspired by them and just as good. It requires a bit of patience and attendance.

FOR 4

400g potatoes, scrubbed and cut into 2cm thick slices

8 artichokes

½ lemon

1 garlic clove

4 small red onions, halved

3 sprigs thyme, leaves picked

1 dried chilli, crumbled

small bunch parsley, chopped

4 tbsp red wine

2 tbsp black olives, pitted

16 slices lardo (optional)

sea salt and extra virgin olive oil

Heat the barbecue. When the charcoal is completely white it is ready.

Clean the artichokes by removing the tough outer leaves, snapping them down. Trim around the base and stem, being aware that this is the prized part, and cutting the stalk to a few centimetres. Then trim away the point of the artichoke and darkest parts of the green leaves. Cut each in half lengthways and use a teaspoon to scoop out the choke. Rub with the cut side of the lemon to stop them discolouring. Slice half of the garlic and insert around the tops of the artichokes. Season with salt.

Parboil the potatoes with the onions in rolling salted water for 6 minutes. Toss with the artichokes, thyme, half the parsley, 2 tablespoons of the wine and another of olive oil while hot.

Place the vegetables on to the grill one by one with tongs in a single layer. Make sure the artichokes are face up with the choke exposed. Turn them after 8 minutes and then regularly after that, keeping the artichokes mostly face up. Cook for a total of about 20 minutes until a few of the outside leaves on the artichokes have blackened and the potatoes have cooked through with golden and darker patches.

Mix the remaining ingredients with a squeeze more of lemon and two tablespoons of oil. Remove the vegetables from the grill and turn in this mixture before serving on a large plate with the lardo draped over, if using. This is equally good with an anchovy and a poached egg.

WHOLE PORCINI IN A PAN

PORCINO INTERO IN PADELLA

I ate porcini at a restaurant in Florence once, stewed slowly with plenty of butter and cheese. The taste remained with me, the pepperiness of undressed rocket leaves against the unctuousness of the creamy mushrooms. The mushrooms need to be of the highest quality. It's something that I make rarely, saving it up as a guilty treat for myself; I've never shared it before.

FOR 1

1 large porcini

1 garlic clove

30g butter

1 thyme sprig, leaves only

25g Parmesan, shaved

handful of rocket, chopped

sea salt, black pepper and extra virgin olive oil

Clean the mushroom by wiping the cap with a damp cloth. Gently break off the leg and peel. Season with salt.

Heat a heavy-based, trustworthy pan over a medium heat with 2 tablespoons of olive oil, the garlic and mushroom leg.

Once hot, when the garlic is slightly coloured, add half the butter, and allow to foam before adding the mushroom cap face down. Leave for 2 minutes before beginning to baste with a tablespoon, tilting the pan so that the butter collects in the edge nearest you and spooning it over the rest of the mushroom. Repeat several times before turning the mushroom over after 5 minutes and adding the thyme. Lower the heat and continue to flick the butter over the mushroom. It has probably soaked in by now so add the rest of the butter.

When another 5 minutes have passed, add half of the cheese over the cap so that it melts.

Sprinkle with the rest of the cheese and eat with the chopped rocket scattered around.

BEETROOTS STEWED WITH LEAVES

BARBABIETOLE ROSSE LESSE

I made this on holiday by the seaside in Suffolk and added lots of wild fennel as it was growing along the track where we were staying. The next day I did just the same thing with a bunch of carrots (bought from the local farm) whose tops were pristine.

It may sound obvious but remember, the fresher the beetroots, the more quickly they cook, so bear this in mind when timing.

FOR 4

bunch beetroots (usually about 5 medium)

2 garlic cloves, sliced

2 red chillies, halved

bunch fennel tops, washed and cut into pieces, or a teaspoon of seeds

sea salt and extra virgin olive oil

Cut the leaves from the beetroots, removing any brown ones, and wash them. Scrub the beetroots well and cut into 1cm slices.

In a wide pan, gently fry the garlic in 4 tablespoons of olive oil, along with the chillies.

When the garlic is golden, add the fennel along with the beetroots. Season well with salt and turn them over. Top with the still-wet beetroot leaves. It might be quite a squeeze, but cover with a lid as best you can.

Allow to steam like this for 25 minutes, turning everything from time to time. You won't need to add any extra liquid, just let the beetroots stew in their own juices. Once the beetroots are cooked to your liking, remove them to a plate and reduce the remaining liquor if needed before pouring over and serving.

PUMPKIN AND PEPPERS
ZUCCA CON PEPERONI

This is something to make at the start of winter, when the pumpkins have ripened and the peppers are still good. Two 'sweet' ingredients but with totally different profiles, it is easy to distinguish the taste of each in this dish.

FOR 4

1kg pumpkin peeled, deseeded and chopped into chunks

1 medium potato, peeled and halved

3 garlic cloves

2 large red peppers, deseeded and chopped quite finely

1 dried chilli

2 plum tomatoes, quartered

bunch basil

sea salt and extra virgin olive oil

In a heavy-based pan, heat 3 tablespoons of oil and then add the pumpkin, potato and garlic with a pinch of salt. Stir over a high heat before adding the peppers and chilli. Continue to cook over a medium heat for a few minutes before adding the tomato and half of the basil, stalks and all.

Cover with a lid and continue to cook over a lower heat. Stir and check once in a while – it should take about 30 minutes to cook. When ready, the edges of the pumpkin and potato will have mushed into each other but there will be a little resistance.

Loosen with some more oil while you test the seasoning and stir in the rest of the basil.

BORLOTTI IN RED WINE
BORLOTTI AL VINO

I buy the best dried pulses I can find: a worthwhile extravagance. It makes a real difference if the beans are from a recent harvest and from an organic grower. If the 'best before' date is two summers away you are looking at a good packet! Putting them on to soak is probably the most labour-intensive stage between you and a fine meal, since beans simply boiled and then doused in olive oil is one of the best things to eat that I know. But here, I have given them a little bit of extra attention. They need nothing else but if you want to, sit them alongside a whole baked fish or a cut of meat; it would be a special occasion.

FOR 4

2 fennel bulbs

sage, parsley, rosemary and thyme sprigs

300g dried borlotti beans, soaked overnight in cold water

½ garlic bulb

75ml extra virgin olive oil

½ bottle red wine

2 fresh chillies

1 tsp sea salt

If the outside layer of the fennel looks stringy remove it, then cut the bulbs into 8 wedges each – vertically, so that the root holds each piece together.

Tie all the herbs together with a piece of string, winding it around so that not too many rosemary needles fall out.

Drain the beans and put everything in a large pan. Top up with water to cover the beans by 5cm. Bring to the boil, cover with a piece of baking paper and simmer for 1½ hours or until soft. (If you prefer baking them, the cooking can be done in the oven on 180°C once the liquid has come to the boil.) Top up with water when necessary, but not so much that you lose the thick creaminess.

These beans are at their best when they sit for a bit before serving.

POTATOES WITH PEPPERS IN VINEGAR

PATATE E PEPERONI ALL'ACETO

This is one of the last dishes that my grandmother taught me. She said that the peppers she remembers from childhood were spicier than they are now, so she would add dried chilli to the sweeter peppers to compensate. This is a potato dish that is easily satisfying enough to eat on its own. If I had to choose something to put with it, it'd be an egg fried with a thin slice of pecorino cheese melting on top.

FOR 2

300g firm potatoes, such as Désirée, Nicola or Linzer, peeled

1 garlic clove, chopped

2 dried chillies, crushed (optional)

2 jarred Red Peppers in Vinegar (page 104), or shop bought, quartered

sea salt and extra virgin olive oil

Slice the potatoes horizontally into rounds 2cm thick. Pour a generous 4 tablespoons of oil into a small frying pan and add the potatoes along with the garlic and crushed chillies. Put a lid on the pan and cook on a medium-high heat.

When you begin to smell the garlic cooking, take off the lid and stir, then add the peppers and replace the lid. Turn the heat down to low and continue cooking for 15 minutes. Season with salt and keep covered until ready to serve. They benefit from sitting around a little before eating.

DRIED PEAS WITH PURPLE SPROUTING BROCCOLI
PISELLI SECCHI CON BROCCOLETTI

This winter dish gives a nod to the smashed broad beans and *cicoria* (Italian green grown for its bitter flavour) from Puglia that I am obsessed with. Cook the dried peas in plenty of water and be patient, letting them smash down on themselves as they cook rather than puréeing in a machine.

FOR 4

250g dried green peas, soaked overnight in cold water with ½ tsp bicarbonate of soda

½ onion, cut into segments

7 garlic cloves

2 celery sticks

1 potato, peeled

3 bay leaves

1kg purple sprouting broccoli

1 tbsp fennel seeds

1 dried chilli

sea salt, black pepper and extra virgin olive oil

Drain the peas and put in a pan of water to cover, with the onion, 5 of the garlic cloves, the celery, potato and bay leaves. Bring to the boil then turn down the heat and simmer until the potatoes and peas are soft. The time this can take varies but around 40 minutes is a good guideline.

When they are soft, turn the heat up, add a pinch of salt and begin to stir with a wooden spoon. Remove the bay leaves. Everything else should begin to mush together. Keep stirring from time to time as it thickens, reducing the heat again to avoid it catching. The consistency you want should be thicker than soup, more like puréed potatoes. When you've achieved this, add a good 3–4 tablespoons of oil, turn off the heat and cover to keep warm. It will thicken as it sits.

Blanch the broccoli in plenty of salted water for 3 minutes. Put 2 tablespoons of olive oil in a pan over a medium heat along with the rest of the garlic, the fennel seeds and chilli. Slowly fry until the garlic is golden and before the spices burn. Use a spoon to remove the garlic but leave the chilli if for nothing but the look. Add the broccoli and continue to cook over a low heat for 5 minutes. Serve with the peas.

TURNIPS AND CHESTNUTS

RAPE E CASTAGNE

When I asked a market trader in Genova what *he* does with turnips, he shrugged his shoulders and muttered that he just fried them like potatoes. Of course I tried this straight away, but the result was limp and greasy with their bitterness amplified. I think they suit pickling or slow-cooking better. This recipe does the classic – pairing something sweet with something bitter.

Cime di rapa literally means turnip tops. If you can find them, add a few. It is even better to buy turnips with tops attached. If you are without turnip tops, use something else (I like frisée lettuce) or skip them, but please make this just the same. A real winter zinger.

FOR 4

250g chestnuts

1kg turnips, peeled and cut into wedges

500g *cime di rapa* (turnip tops), washed and chopped

1 garlic clove, halved

bunch sage, leaves only

100g jarred tomatoes, drained, or Pommarola (page 100)

175ml white wine

salted ricotta (optional)

sea salt, black pepper and extra virgin olive oil

Prepare the chestnuts by scoring and boiling them for 5 minutes, or microwaving on high for 3 minutes, then peeling.

Bring a large pan of salted water to the boil and cook the turnips for 5 minutes, followed by the greens for a similar time.

Fry the garlic in another large pan over a high heat with 3 tablespoons of olive oil, adding the sage just before the garlic starts to turn golden, about 4 minutes. Then add the chestnuts and tomatoes. Use a spoon to help break up the tomatoes.

Add the turnips and wine and bring to the boil. Top up with roughly 200ml water and proceed to cook over a medium heat for about 25 minutes. At this point, add the green tops and continue to cook for only a few minutes more before turning off the heat and adding a couple of tablespoons of olive oil.

Serve on a flat platter with salted ricotta flaked over, if you like.

WHOLE SPELT WITH FRESH PEAS

FARRO E PISELLI

This is neither a salad nor a soup but a stand-alone dish that is a halfway house between the two. The cheese adds a melty, stringy, sparkling luxury to what would otherwise be 100 per cent wholesome. If you find pearled spelt you could consider not soaking it so long, but I think you'll find a head start in its softening a good thing either way.

FOR 4

1 garlic clove, chopped

1 carrot, diced

1 celery stick, diced

40g pancetta, diced

1 onion, diced

2 rosemary sprigs, leaves picked and chopped

150g farro (whole spelt) soaked overnight in cold water

300g shelled fresh or frozen peas

handful of basil leaves

100g fontina, diced

sea salt, black pepper and extra virgin olive oil

Put the garlic, carrot, celery, pancetta and half of the onion in a large pan along with 2 tablespoons of oil and gently sweat. Let it cook for 15 minutes on a low heat, taking care that it doesn't catch. Then add the rosemary.

Drain the farro and add to the pan, covering with water by at least 5cm. Bring to the boil and simmer for 30 minutes. Test to see how soft the farro is. If it's still hard, top up the water and continue to cook until relatively dry.

Meanwhile, cook the rest of the onion in a separate pan with a pinch of salt and a little oil until translucent. Add the peas with most of the basil leaves, cover with a lid and cook for 15 minutes – what the peas will have lost in their vivid colour they will have gained in flavour. If the peas dry, add a spot of water (this is, however, unlikely if you use frozen).

Mix the peas into the farro with the cheese. Tear in some more basil and add a tablespoon or two of olive oil.

Check the seasoning and pour into a serving bowl. This is best once cooled a little so that the cheese thickens.

RUNNER BEANS, PANCETTA AND ALMONDS
FAGIOLINI RAMPICANTI, PANCETTA E MANDORLE

This is a treat all round. Just like a good carbonara it's the slow and careful cooking of the pancetta or guanciale that makes this more special. The aromatic juniper adds interest and is often used in making pancetta.

FOR 4

175g almonds

100g thick slice pancetta or guanciale, sliced

8 juniper berries

1kg runner beans

1 dried chilli, crushed

sea salt and extra virgin olive oil

Preheat the oven to 170°C/fan 150°C/gas 3.

Coat the almonds in ½ teaspoon of oil with a pinch of salt and toast in the oven for about 30 minutes. Remove from the oven and allow to cool, then blitz or coarsely grate.

Sauté the pancetta pieces in a tablespoon of olive oil. Do this over a medium-low heat until some fat has rendered out of the meat and it turns crispy on the outside. This takes longer than you think. Add the juniper berries and chilli halfway through.

While you are waiting for the pancetta to turn crispy, top, tail and string the runner beans. Slice lengthways and cook in boiling salted water for 4 minutes, then drain and keep warm.

When the meat is crisp, remove the juniper and discard. Then mix in the beans and almonds and serve right away.

LAYERED AUBERGINE

MELANZANE A STRATI

Having become accustomed to cooking aubergines without salting them, because of using the round mauve type, I had forgotten how good the old long ones are. For this recipe it is they that are much the best – full of character. They need salting, yes, but it means that they are soft and ready for this straightforward method. The texture of the thin slices against each other makes this dish special. These aubergines are good with another vegetable, or with a simple grilled meat chop or sausage.

FOR 3

2 aubergines

2 bay leaves

zest and juice of 1 lemon

1 rosemary sprig, leaves only

10 sage leaves, chopped

2 parsley sprigs, chopped

1 garlic clove, chopped

½ dried chilli, deseeded and sliced

200g breadcrumbs

grated Parmesan (or whatever hard cheese you have in the fridge)

butter

sea salt and extra virgin olive oil

Slice the aubergines thinly. Salt and leave for an hour or so in a colander for the bitter juices to drain out. Wash them under the tap and pat dry.

Preheat the oven to 220°C/fan 200°C/gas 7 and line a baking tray with baking paper. Toss the aubergines with a little olive oil.

Cut the bay leaves in half, removing the central stem, and chop very finely. Then chop again and again. Squeeze a little lemon juice over the rosemary and sage and chop as well. Put the chopped bay leaves, rosemary and parsley in a bowl, grate over the lemon zest and mix in the garlic and chilli, along with a pinch of salt. Stir in the breadcrumbs and Parmesan.

Sprinkle some of the breadcrumb mix on the baking tray and arrange a third of the aubergines on top in a shape of your choice. Then scatter more of the crumb mix and a few small pieces of butter, before adding another layer of aubergine. Continue, finishing with a layer of the breadcrumb mix and butter.

Loosely cover with foil and bake for 30 minutes. If not golden on top bake for a further 5 minutes uncovered.

This often looks best inverted onto a plate.

PESCE CARNE UOVA

FISH, MEAT AND EGGS

I have found it really hard to write an introduction to this chapter. What have lamb chops in tin foil and white asparagus and eggs got in common? Why did I choose to group them together? Is it because I believe them to be 'main dishes' around which every other dish plays second fiddle? Are they complete meals in their own right? I think it is best explained by describing how we eat at home on a day-to-day basis. Most nights, we cook with what we have in the fridge or store cupboard. This is partly to do with time: small children combined with a busy working life. In my family, we have a weekly delivery of vegetables we work through according to what comes in the box. We have packets of pasta on the go and usually bread to get through. Our 'daily' fish is canned anchovies or tuna, not fresh. And similarly with meat – it is cured that we have most often (pancetta, ham, lardons), using it as flavouring rather than the star.

So the recipes in this chapter represent times we would go out to buy something a bit out of the ordinary. Or find ourselves in special circumstances with, say, access to amazing tomatoes (in sunny Italy, obviously) with which to transform an everyday frittata into something really special. If we were staying with my parents in Tuscany, they would be the kinds of things we would make after a visit to an interesting food market before carrying them down to my grandmother for Sunday lunch. They are the sorts of dishes that would represent to her a degree of luxury and elegance.

Here you will also find a few sauces. It is not unusual for me to begin with preparing one of them and then basing the rest of the meal around it rather than vice-versa.

If you are going to pair the dishes with anything, make it plain; bread or a simple salad or boiled vegetable. Enjoy the sourcing of the ingredients and the cooking. This is meant to be for when you have a bit of time on your hands and are choosing to spend it cooking for the people you love.

CREAMY SMOKED HADDOCK

EGLEFINO MANTECATO

Elizabeth David wrote in her classic *Italian Food*, published in 1954, that salt cod wouldn't catch on in Britain and suggested using smoked haddock instead. With that in mind, I propose this smoked haddock *mantecato*. *Mantecato* simply means creamy, or to cook until creamy. The addition of potatoes balances out the smokiness of the haddock, while making it possibly more reminiscent of fish pie than something Venetian, but in a good way. Serve with plain polenta, on toast or with crunchy endives or similar.

FOR 6

100g fluffy potatoes (you don't want a waxy variety here), peeled

3 garlic cloves

500g smoked haddock, boned, skinned and finely chopped

100–120ml extra virgin olive oil

Boil the potatoes in unsalted water with the garlic cloves until the garlic is completely softened and mellow in flavour, about 20 minutes.

Drain the spuds and return them to the hot saucepan. Add the fish with 2 tablespoons of water. Continue to stir over a low heat.

Use a wooden spoon as you begin to add the oil, whipping the mixture as you go. This is much easier here than it would be with salt cod. Keep adding the oil in a stream, still whipping and pausing every so often to catch your breath. Try to take about 8 minutes to slowly use up all the oil. It's a lot of oil – you can use less but it is meant to be a rich dish.

CUTTLEFISH STEW BAKED ON TOAST

STUFATO DI SEPPIE AL FORNO

Squid has become expensive. I prefer the more buttery cuttlefish. For the moment it's still cheaper, and stands up well in dishes like this. It is available in many sizes. The cooking time indicated below is for medium fish. Small fish I'd cook whole. Definitely have your fishmonger clean it for you – the black ink gets everywhere.

FOR 6

800g cuttlefish, cleaned

1 red onion, diced

2 celery sticks, diced

1 carrot, diced

3 garlic cloves, 2 diced and 1 left whole

1 dried chilli

5 parsley sprigs, chopped

6 sage leaves

2 bay leaves

250ml red wine

250g jarred tomatoes, passata or Pommarola (page 100)

600g chard, washed

6 thick slices sourdough bread

75g coarsely grated pecorino

sea salt, black pepper and extra virgin olive oil

Check over the cuttlefish to make sure they are clean and that the beaks have been removed. Cut into a few pieces.

Heat 3 tablespoons of olive oil in a pan over a moderate heat and begin to cook the *soffritto* – the diced vegetables, parsley and the chilli. Season and add the sage and bay leaves and continue to cook. When the onion is translucent add the red wine, and begin to reduce. Once halved in volume, add the tomatoes and bring to the boil.

Preheat the oven to 190°C/fan 170°C/gas 5.

Add the cuttlefish to the sauce and simmer for 40 minutes until soft. In the meantime, boil the chard in another pan of boiling water for a couple of minutes and roast the bread in an ovenproof dish, turning it over to toast both sides. When toasted, rub the bread on one side with the remaining garlic clove.

Drain the chard, season and drizzle with oil then scatter around the bread in the ovenproof dish. Once the cuttlefish are tender and the sauce is much reduced, pour over the bread and scatter with the cheese.

Bake in the oven for 10 minutes until the sauce has soaked into the bread and the cheese is golden.

BABY OCTOPUS AND PEAS

POLIPETTI E PISELLI

I use frozen octopus because the fresh ones I find here are the single-sucker type and are never satisfactory. If you cannot find small ones, the exact same thing can be done with a whole, large octopus. Chop it into pieces and increase the cooking time in the first stage. Be careful with the salt at first – octopus becomes salty easily. Serve this by itself as a short course in a longer meal. I'd find it hard to eat this without bread to soak up some juices and eventually scrape the bowl out with.

FOR 4

1kg frozen baby octopuses, defrosted

1 red onion, finely sliced

2 garlic cloves

3 bay leaves

2 dried chillies

50g small black olives, pitted

300g shelled peas

600g new potatoes, peeled and cut into 1cm dice

175ml dry wine (white or red)

sea salt and extra virgin olive oil

Run the otopuses under the tap then transfer to a heavy-based pan (a casserole dish would be best) and coat with a few tablespoons of oil. Add the onion, garlic, bay leaves and chillies, cover with a piece of baking paper and the lid and place over a high heat.

Once everything is hot and cooking, turn down the heat and allow the octopuses to cook in their own juices for 15 minutes. Uncover and add the olives, peas, potatoes and wine. Bring to a simmer and continue cooking until the peas and octopuses are soft and yielding, about 20 minutes more.

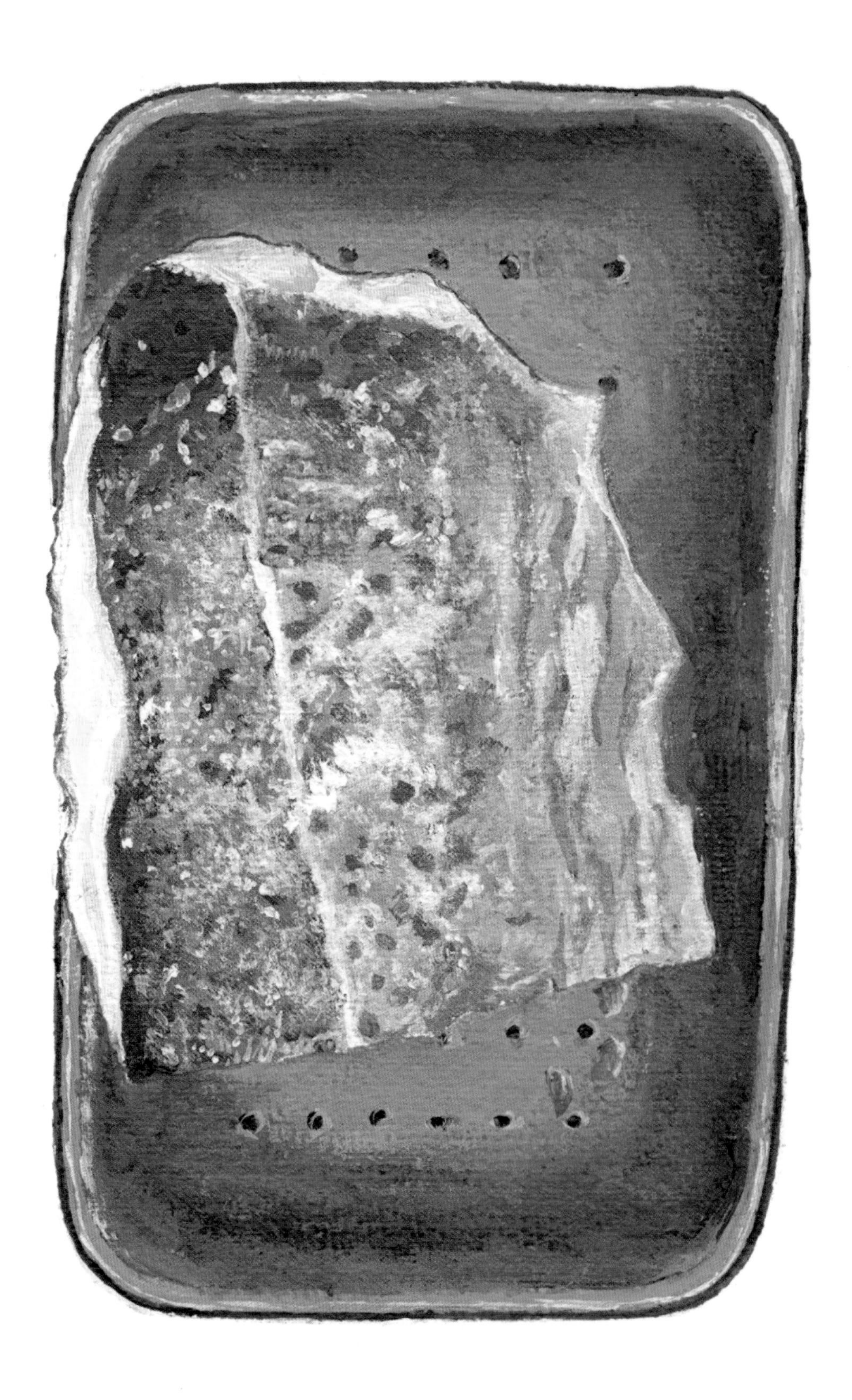

SALT COD | BACCALÁ

My father still calls me '*baccalà*' – salt cod – if I do something clumsy or stupid. I have no idea where it comes from but as the recipient of this barb, it feels both insulting and endearing at the same time. Similar insults, which I fully intend to pass on to my own children, include '*sacco di patate*' – sack of potatoes – for lazy or, the ultimate, '*stoccafisso*' – stockfish – for stubborn or immovable.

Historically, cod was dried, making stockfish, before it was salted. Proper aficionados prefer the simple dried, stronger-tasting cod. It's much trickier to prepare and, as far as I'm concerned, inferior to the mighty salt cod. I believe fresh cod is transformed by salting, and it is super-simple to salt your own. It is also dried after salting so that it lasts, but I find that a quick salting transforms it enough for me at home. I love the contradiction of it; rich and robust, it can still be delicate – and, while relatively cheap, it has a hint of mystery and luxury. And what does preserved fish – or preserved anything – represent but the anticipation and promise of good meals to come?

Doing it myself, it is easier to be sure that the cod used has been sustainably fished. It is absolutely possible to substitute other fish, but cod reigns supreme in the following recipes. Make more than you need and freeze a couple of portions for another recipe.

I love that a method perfected by the Vikings became a mainstay of Mediterranean cooking. The list of famous dishes is long. In Venice, *baccalà mantecato* or *alla vicentina* would be the typical choice: two hugely important dishes. Further south, boiled and then doused in olive oil strongly flavoured with garlic and dried chillies might be more typical. All over Italy, salted fish is still the fish of choice a long way from harbour.

A lasting image I have of Rose Gray is her beating salt cod wrapped in a tea towel over the kitchen counter. She had brought the fish back from Lisbon and used it to trial salting our own cod. As John Cleese set about his Mini Cooper in *Fawlty Towers*, so Rose, in comic turn, gave that *baccalà* a wonderful tenderising.

SALT COD SALAD WITH PEPPERS IN VINEGAR

INSALATA DI BACCALÀ CON PEPERONI SOTT'ACETO

There are three options for the cod. 1. Use purchased dried, salted, bona-fide *baccalà* washed in several changes of fresh water over three days. 2. Use fresh cod that you have sprinkled with salt the day before and then washed. 3. (Much lighter) soak the fresh cod in a brine of 10g of salt with a litre of water for 15 minutes, even this firms the fish more than you might expect.

If you can't find the exact mix of greens that I have used in the recipe then mix it up with others, but beware of the strongest brassicas as they might overpower the dish.

FOR 4

1kg salt cod fillet, soaked

200g Red Peppers in Vinegar (page 104), chopped

zest and juice of ½ lemon

100g green olives

4 parsley sprigs, coarsely chopped

extra virgin olive oil

Bring a pan of water to the boil and add the cod. Unless it is very thick and very dry I prefer not to overcook it, finding that 5–10 minutes is usually enough. Remove it from the water with a slotted spoon and check it is done by gently pulling it apart to so that it just flakes without resistance. As soon as it's cool enough to handle, flake the flesh away from the skin and remove any bones. Try to keep the cod in nice, large pieces.

Place on a plate and dress with the peppers, lemon zest and juice, the olives, parsley and finally the oil. Taste for seasoning – but I doubt it will need any more salt.

SALT COD COOKED OVER POTATOES WITH GREENS

BACCALÀ CON PATATE E VERDURE

This was another of my grandmother's favourites. It makes your lips curl with the salt of the fish and the vinegar from the peppers, even more so than the salt and vinegar on traditionally fried fish.

FOR 4

2 garlic cloves, sliced

1 dried chilli

½ head celery, preferably with root and all the leaves, quartered

2 bay leaves

100g cherry tomatoes

500g medium potatoes, peeled

bunch *cicoria di catalogna* (puntarelle), washed

1 head escarole, or frisée, washed

600g salt cod

sea salt, black pepper and extra virgin olive oil

In a large heavy-based pan, cook the garlic in a thick glug of olive oil over a medium heat. When it starts to colour, add the chilli and a pinch of salt. Quite quickly follow with the celery, leaves and all, bay leaves, tomatoes and potatoes. Cover with water.

Once it simmers, add the rest of the greens, give it all a stir and put on a lid. Don't worry if the greens aren't totally covered, they'll collapse soon. Cook for 25 minutes over a low heat or until the potatoes are almost done, keeping the level of the water just below that of the ingredients in the pan.

Add the cod, skin side up, cover and gently simmer. The cod should cook within 10 minutes if it was lightly salted. Thicker pieces that have been more heavily salted could take between 15 and 20 minutes; just keep an eye on it and check its resistance when prodded by a fork.

Turn off the heat and let the pan sit with the lid on for a few minutes in order for the flavours to intermingle and the cod to relax. It can sit for much longer if need be. Set the table with spoons and forks and serve the cod in bowls, covered with the broth and vegetables.

FISH BALLS

POLPETTE DI PESCE

This was Dad's idea. He's been making meatballs with equal parts vegetable and mince. This is the fish version. Although very different, mackerel, herrings or swordfish work equally well in this recipe. Skip the greens and tomato bit if you like.

FOR 4

100g old bread, crusts removed
250g oily fish, skinned
2 salted anchovy fillets
100g courgette, grated
1 egg
Scratch of nutmeg
small bunch parsley, chopped
breadcrumbs
40g salted ricotta
400g *cime di rapa* or chard
1 garlic clove, sliced
1 tsp fennel seeds
100g cherry tomatoes
sea salt and extra virgin olive oil

Soak the bread in cold water. Chop the fish up into small pieces, removing any bones and put into the bowl of a mixer with the anchovies. Squeeze and add the bread. Whizz until well combined but stop short of it becoming a paste.

In a bowl, mix the courgette with the blitzed fish, egg, nutmeg, parsley, cheese and a small pinch of salt. Once mixed, begin to shape into small, walnut-sized balls. Roll in the breadcrumbs and set aside in the fridge until needed.

Boil the *cime di rapa* in water for 5 minutes then drain. Fry the garlic with the fennel seeds until sticky and then tear in the tomatoes and add a pinch of salt. Toss the drained greens into the pan and continue to cook over a brisk flame for 5 minutes.

Heat 4 tablespoons of oil in a frying pan and add the balls one by one. Cook for 3 minutes on one side before turning them. They should be golden and crisp on all sides, so keep moving them around. Cook for about 8 minutes in total.

Remove to a plate lined with kitchen paper for a quick blot before serving with the greens.

POACHED FISH
IL PESCE LESSO

This is an extremely simple process but very worth including. While the delicate white-fleshed fish, such as halibut, might be considered some of the best to poach, there isn't to my mind a fish that poaches badly. Few extra ingredients are necessary as the game is not to mask the delicate flavour. I particularly like to poach large steaks of fish. One herb and a little wine is enough, especially if it's going to be served with something stronger-tasting. I use the stalks of the herbs rather than the leaves because they are less inclined to turn the water green yet have a good flavour, and then I can use the leaves in a complementary sauce or another dish.

FOR 2

2 x 200g fish steaks

a few basil or parsley sprigs, stalks only (leaves reserved for something else)

50ml white wine

200ml water

generous pinch sea salt and 4 black peppercorns

Put everything into a pan with a tight-fitting lid. It doesn't matter if the level of the liquid only partially covers the fish.

Bring to a simmer over a medium-high heat and cook for 5 minutes, then turn off the heat but leave the fish in the pan with the lid on for another 5 minutes.

I like to peel off the skin before serving but it's not obligatory.

TUNA COOKED IN LENTILS

TONNO COTTO NELLE LENTICCHIE

Meaty tuna, meaty lentils – a great match.

FOR 4

200g dried lentils

1 tablespoon flour

1 tsp coriander seeds, crushed

350g thick-cut tuna steaks (sustainably sourced), cut in 3cm cubes

2 garlic cloves

200g cherry tomatoes, halved

small bunch basil, leaves only

40g butter

1 lemon

sea salt, black pepper and extra virgin olive oil

Rinse the lentils and cook them in a pan of water until al dente, about 20 minutes. When cooked, drain their water.

Season the flour with salt and the coriander. Lightly dust the tuna pieces. Put 3 tablespoons of oil in a wide pan and fry the garlic until golden. Remove the garlic and add the tuna. Turn quickly and add the tomatoes and basil to the pan, followed by the lentils. Keep them on a low heat and under supervision as you prepare the tuna.

Turn off the heat then add the butter on top and leave in the residual heat for 8 minutes, basting with the lentils. Squeeze over the fresh lemon and season with black pepper before serving.

BREAM IN VINEGAR AND BREADCRUMBS

ORATA IMPANATA CON L'ACETO

Cooking fish like this in crumbs really holds the moisture in and is more delicate than deep-frying. It is very straightforward and lovely to share a whole fish, but if you prefer to use smaller pieces they would also work well. John Dory would be a good alternative if you can't find bream. This reminds me of holidays and driving back from the beach, stopping en route at a favourite roadside canteen where a Sicilian ex-fisherman cooks us fish always coated in breadcrumbs. If he serves it with anything at all it might be a ubiquitous but nonetheless delicious tomato salad or grilled courgettes.

FOR 2

1 1kg bream

50ml red wine vinegar

1 rosemary sprig, or other herb, chopped

flour for dusting

1 egg, whisked

200g breadcrumbs

sea salt, black pepper and extra virgin olive oil

I like to butterfly the fish from the back but regular fillets are fine as well. It is tricky but you will get the hang of it. This is how you do it. Scale the fish. Cut off the fins and head. Pull out the innards and rinse the fish. Use a knife to cut down the ridge of the fin on the back along the length of the fish and continue to fillet. Keep the knife angled in towards the bone so as not to cut through the flesh. Cut until the bone is released from the flesh and you can open the fish out. Repeat this on the other side of the backbone so that it is completely removed from the fish. If there are any obvious remaining bones remove them and you can pin-bone the fish if you like. Wash the fish again and pat dry with kitchen paper.

Put the fish in the vinegar and sprinkle with the rosemary and some salt. Leave to soak in the fridge for an hour or so, then pat dry.

Lightly dust the fish with flour before dredging in the egg and then the breadcrumbs. Make sure it is covered all over.

Heat 5 tablespoons of oil in a large frying pan. Add the fish away from you so as to avoid any splashback. Keep the heat at medium, allowing the egg mixture to fizz around the edges of the fish and crisp slowly without burning. After 4 minutes carefully turn the fish over using tongs and cook on the other side for another 4 minutes. Use a skewer to check that the fish is cooked through.

Briefly blot on kitchen paper before serving.

BREAM IN A PAN

ORATA IN PADELLA

The flavour is totally different using fresh rather than dried porcini but both are worth making. *Mare e monti* – land and sea.

FOR 4

2 very ripe tomatoes

1 garlic clove, sliced

20g dried porcini, reconstituted for 15 minutes in hot water, or 200g fresh porcini

1 x 1.5kg bream

small bunch parsley

75ml white wine

knob of butter

sea salt, black pepper and extra virgin olive oil

Slice the tomatoes into wedges and squeeze if excessively juicy to remove some of the liquid.

Put a tablespoon of olive oil in a pan big enough to hold the fish and fry the garlic with the porcini, whether you are using dried (drain and reserve the liquid) or fresh. Once the garlic is slightly translucent, add the reserved mushroom soaking water (if you are using dried porcini). Then add the tomatoes and cook for 10 minutes over a lowish heat.

Scale and clean the bream. Cut off the fins with stout scissors – this will make serving the fish easier (if you remember, you could have your fishmonger do this for you). If you have a lid for your pan then great, otherwise you can make your own by lining a piece of foil with baking paper and crimping the edges together.

Take the pan off the heat. Season the fish and place in among the porcini, turning it over so that it is flavoured all over. Add the parsley and wine then clamp over your lid and return to the heat.

Cook for 8 minutes, basting from time to time, then turn the fish over, adding the butter and a splash of water if needed, and continue to cook for a further 5 minutes, or until the fish gives at the thickest part when pierced with a skewer.

LEAN BEEF IN OLIVE OIL
BRASATO DI MANZO

This dish adds richness thanks to the large amount of olive oil. Halve it if you have to, but don't remove it altogether. I like to save money but I'm not going to prattle on about the cheap cuts; in fact I'm going to try this with fillet, in a shallower pan with less liquid, a shorter cooking time and leaving it just pink. Serve with something on the blander, earthier side that will benefit from the rich sauce.

FOR 4

1.4kg lean braising beef joint

10 anchovy fillets

15 bay leaves

8 garlic cloves, some sliced

1 tbsp flour

200ml extra virgin olive oil

2 onions, chopped

2 celery sticks, cut into 6

1 heaped tbsp salted capers

2 lemons

chopped fresh parsley

sea salt and black pepper (including some whole corns)

Use the point of a knife to cut 15 small pockets in the meat. Lace these with pieces of the anchovies, a bay leaf, some slivers of garlic and plenty of whole peppercorns. Space them out and take your time, it's rewarding when it ends up looking good.

Flour and salt the meat. Heat 2 tablespoons of the oil in a heavy-based pan with a tight-fitting lid and brown the meat carefully on all sides. Fit the onions, remaining garlic, the celery and any leftover anchovies along with the capers around the meat. Don't worry about browning these too.

Add the rest of the oil and pour in water to almost cover the beef, about 400ml in my pot. Add the juice of one of the lemons. Bring to a simmer and cover with a piece of baking paper and the lid.

Continue to simmer for at least 2½ hours. Check from time to time and add water should it become necessary. When the meat is totally soft, almost falling apart, carefully remove from the pan and put on a warm plate. Reduce the remaining liquid and then pass through a food mill, or blitz the vegetables to make a sauce, adding parsley, more lemon juice and pepper to taste.

Slice the beef and serve with the sauce spooned over.

PORK CHOPS WITH QUINCE AND VINEGAR

BRACIOLE DI MAIALE CON MELA COTOGNA

What is so compelling is the hot, sweet quinces in combination with the fatty meat. Cook the quinces in advance to keep the eventual preparation to a minimum.

FOR 2

1 onion, sliced

1 garlic clove

1 quince, peeled and sliced into 2cm discs

50ml red wine vinegar

2 pork chops, lightly trimmed

2 tbsp fresh oregano

sea salt, black pepper and extra virgin olive oil

Sweat the onion and garlic with a tablespoon of oil in a small saucepan over a medium heat. When soft, add the quince and turn up the heat. Fry for a few minutes, keeping a watchful eye on the onion. Then add the vinegar, allowing it to boil and reduce. Then add water to cover. Bring to the boil and simmer until the quince is soft and the liquid is much reduced. This might take 30–40 minutes.

Once the quince is cooked, heat a frying pan with a little oil to hot but not smoking. Season the chops on all sides with salt and the oregano, reserving a few leaves for the end. Sear the chops on one side for 5 minutes before turning and cooking for another 5 minutes. Add the quinces with all their juice. Allow the pan to deglaze, turn off the heat and make sure everything is covered on all sides. Leave to rest for 5 minutes. If you prefer, you can of course cook your chops for less time so that they are pinker.

RABBIT ROASTED IN PARMESAN

CONIGLIO COTTO IN PARMIGIANO

Many may be put off cooking rabbit but they shouldn't be. Success is guaranteed with farmed rabbits which are much more tender than wild. I could write a whole book of rabbit recipes – it's incredibly versatile. This recipe came to us on a trip to Emilia-Romagna. We ate it washed down with Lambrusco. This recipe has two stages, with much of the preparation happening in advance of the cooking, so it's a good one to make if you're having friends over. I serve this with spinach as it pairs so well with Parmesan.

FOR 4

1 farmed rabbit

2 celery sticks, chopped

1 carrot, chopped

1 garlic bulb, halved

5 bay leaves, chopped

2 tbsp chopped rosemary

500ml whole milk

200g Parmesan, grated

sea salt, black pepper and extra virgin olive oil

The night before, clean and wash the rabbit, season and set aside in a bowl. Cover the rabbit with the chopped vegetables and garlic, herbs and milk. Refrigerate overnight.

The next day, preheat the oven to 180°C/fan 160°C/gas 4 and line a roasting tray with baking paper.

Take the rabbit from the milk and cover it all over in the Parmesan. Put the rabbit in the prepared tray and roast for 2½ hours, turning after the first hour and then again after the second.

The rabbit is ready when it obtains a ruddy, rusty colour.

Joint the meat before serving.

SLOW-BOILED MEAT
LESSO DI CARNE

Poaching is a straightforward if underused method of cooking. It doesn't have the macho glamour of roasting or grilling over wood. But what it lacks in looks you can make up for in accompaniments.

This is less of a recipe and more of a guide to how to transform a tough, sinewy cut of meat into something soft and yielding. Tie into shape if you like. The major rule is to cook super-slowly after introducing the meat into boiling water. A gentle simmer will transform the meat into something you will want to serve with a complementary sauce (see pages 204–209). Steer clear of the prime cuts, but most of the rest of the animal is applicable here, especially good beef-wise is brisket, top side, short ribs, feather blade or tongue.

FOR 6

1.5kg beef top side

5 litres water

small handful sea salt

1 tsp black peppercorns

3 celery sticks

1 onion

1 leek

1 garlic bulb, halved

10 herb sprigs – thyme and/or parsley, sage, bay leaves, fennel

1 tbsp juniper and/or 5 cloves or other spices (optional)

For the very best result sprinkle salt all over the meat a day or two ahead, but this is by no means absolutely necessary.

Bring everything bar the meat to the boil in a large stockpot filled with salted water. Bear in mind the quantity of salt you are adding, especially if you have salted the cut ahead of time.

Add the meat to the pot and bring back to a soft simmer, then allow everything to tick over for a long time. If it boils too fast, the meat will stay tough and tasteless. Skim any impurities away as and when they rise to the surface.

Check after 3 hours. There should be little resistance when a skewer or knife is inserted into the meat.

Slice before serving with olive oil as a minimum but, even better accompany with a sauce. The broth you can taste and keep for making risotto or soup another time.

MEAT IN TOMATO SAUCE

CARNE AL SUGO

'In sauce' is an excellent way of cooking anything, especially meat. Don't feel you have to stick to beef, veal and pork either. It works with rabbit or poultry, jointed first. On family days we use the resulting sauce to coat pasta as a starter and follow with the meat. Having already eaten pasta we often serve this with a simple green salad to follow. It couldn't be easier. This is the smell that used to drive me crazy on a Sunday, wafting from the balconies when I was on exchange in Italy and abandoned by student friends who had all rushed home for something similar.

FOR 6

1kg beef for braising

3 garlic cloves, sliced

pinch dried chilli

150ml dry white wine

650g good-quality passata plus 800g jarred tomatoes, or 1.5kg Pommarola (page 100)

small bunch basil

sea salt and extra virgin olive oil

Cut the meat into thick slices about 4cm across. Heat 2 tablespoons of olive oil in a large heavy-based pan and roughly brown the meat – you don't have to be too precise about it. Add the garlic halfway through and watch that it doesn't burn. Add the dried chilli and follow with the wine.

When the wine has mostly evaporated, add the tomatoes and basil. Bring to the boil then turn down the heat and simmer for about 2 hours until the meat is soft and the sauce reduced. Ladle the thickened sauce over freshly cooked pasta if you want to indulge in a full meal, allowing the meat to rest while you have your first course.

POACHED CHICKEN
POLLO LESSO

Here's an idea for a quick poached chicken supper that is always popular at home. It's an absurdly simple one-pot meal that might be a gateway to other boiled meat dishes. A no-fuss recipe that is health-giving, adaptable and extremely comforting.

FOR 2

6 medium potatoes, peeled
2 carrots, peeled
2 celery sticks, peeled
½ shallot
2 garlic cloves
4 parsley sprigs
1 bay leaf
½ fennel bulb
4 junipers
2 chicken legs
150g chard
Sea salt and black pepper

Put all the vegetables in a large pan and add the garlic, herbs and spices. Cover with water and bring to the boil. Cook for 30 minutes before adding the chicken, seasoning and bringing back to the boil. Simmer for 5 minutes, then add the chard; it doesn't have to be completely submerged. Continue simmering for another 15–20 minutes. Turn off the heat and leave in the water for 10 minutes before checking that the chicken is cooked through by piercing with the point of a knife – if the juices run clear it's cooked.

Peel the skin from the chicken before serving with the potatoes and chard – the other vegetables tend to have little or no flavour left. Sometimes I like to serve with a sauce made of a potato and broth (see page 168).

ROAST CHICKEN AND POTATOES
POLLO E PATATE AL FORNO

The only problem with roasting a chicken is that I am expected to carve. To be honest, I'd rather wash up. This method has all the benefit of cooking the chicken whole but I get to cut it up earlier and then relax.

FOR 4

1 x 1.5kg chicken

5 garlic cloves

1 large bulb of fennel, cut into 8

20g dried porcini

150ml white wine

1kg new potatoes, scrubbed and halved

200g old bread

1 bunch of basil, leaves picked

sea salt, black pepper and extra virgin olive oil

Preheat the oven to 200°C/fan 180°C/gas 6.

Season the chicken inside and out with salt. Place in a high-sided pan that will fit the bird tightly. Add the garlic cloves, fennel, porcini and wine and a rough 100ml of water. Bring to the boil and then turn down to simmer.

Cover with a lid askew and leave to cook on a moderate heat for about 30 minutes, turning it over after 20.

Meanwhile, prepare the potatoes by lightly seasoning with salt and tossing in a teaspoon of olive oil. Place on a spacious roasting tray and cook for 40 minutes or until golden and cooked.

Remove the chicken from the pan. If there is a lot of juice left, reduce for 5 minutes over a high heat. Chop the bread into large cubes and toss with a little oil. Use a good pair of scissors to cut the backbone out of the chicken. Cut the legs away and then the drumstick from the thigh. Cut the breast still on the bone into several pieces. Arrange the chicken in and around the cooked potatoes with the bread and fresh basil. Spoon over the sauce from the pan and return the tray to the oven for 10 minutes before serving.

PORK WITH PEPPERS

MAIALE E PATATE AL FORNO

This is a slow-cooked version inspired by the more traditional quick-cooked pork belly or pork chops and pickled pepper combo.

FOR 4

1.5kg pork shoulder, boned and rind removed

8 cloves garlic, peeled

1 branch rosemary, picked and chopped

1 branch sage, picked

1 jar of peppers in vinegar, bought or homemade (see page 104)

100ml dry white wine

Sea salt, black pepper, extra virgin olive oil

Pre-heat the oven to 200°C/fan 180°C/gas mark 6.

Season the meat well with salt. In a large, heavy ovenproof pot, heat 1 tablespoon of olive oil and sear the pork joint turning until all sides are coloured and some of fat has rendered out. Remove from the pot with tongs and discard the fat.

Return the pot to the heat and add the whole garlic cloves. Allow them to fry for a minute before adding the seared pork and the herbs.

Add the peppers, tearing them into pieces as you put them around and on the pork. Add the vinegar from the jar (if I use bought I often add a bit of extra wine vinegar for good luck) and the wine. Season with black pepper and allow to boil before covering with a piece of greaseproof paper and the lid. Transfer to the oven and cook for 3 hours, checking and basting after an hour and then every 30 minutes. Add water if the pot looks in danger of drying out – I usually find it needs a mug of water around 2 hours in.

Remove from the oven. Slice or tear apart the meat and serve covered with the resulting tart pepper sauce.

LAMB CHOPS IN TIN FOIL

COSTOLETTE DI AGNELLO IN CARTOCCIO

This is a spring thing. It has the benefit of everything being cooked together, and the added bonus of little washing-up.

FOR 4

1 tbsp thyme leaves

1–2 red onions (such as Tropea), finely sliced

8 lamb chops

80g green beans, topped and tailed

350g broad beans in their pods, shelled

2 ripe plum tomatoes, cut into strips

8 courgette flowers

16 olives of choice

4 salted anchovy fillets (optional)

sea salt, black pepper and extra virgin olive oil

Preheat the oven to 200°C/fan 180°C/gas 6.

Prepare four large squares of foil by brushing them with a little oil in the middle. Scatter over half of the thyme and a few onion slices and season with salt and pepper. Place the lamb chops on top and season again, adding the remaining thyme and onion mixed with the other vegetables, olives and anchovies, if using. Cover with another square of foil and roll the edges together on all sides towards the chop in the centre. Bake for 20 minutes.

Serve the foil parcels on plates for everyone to open their own.

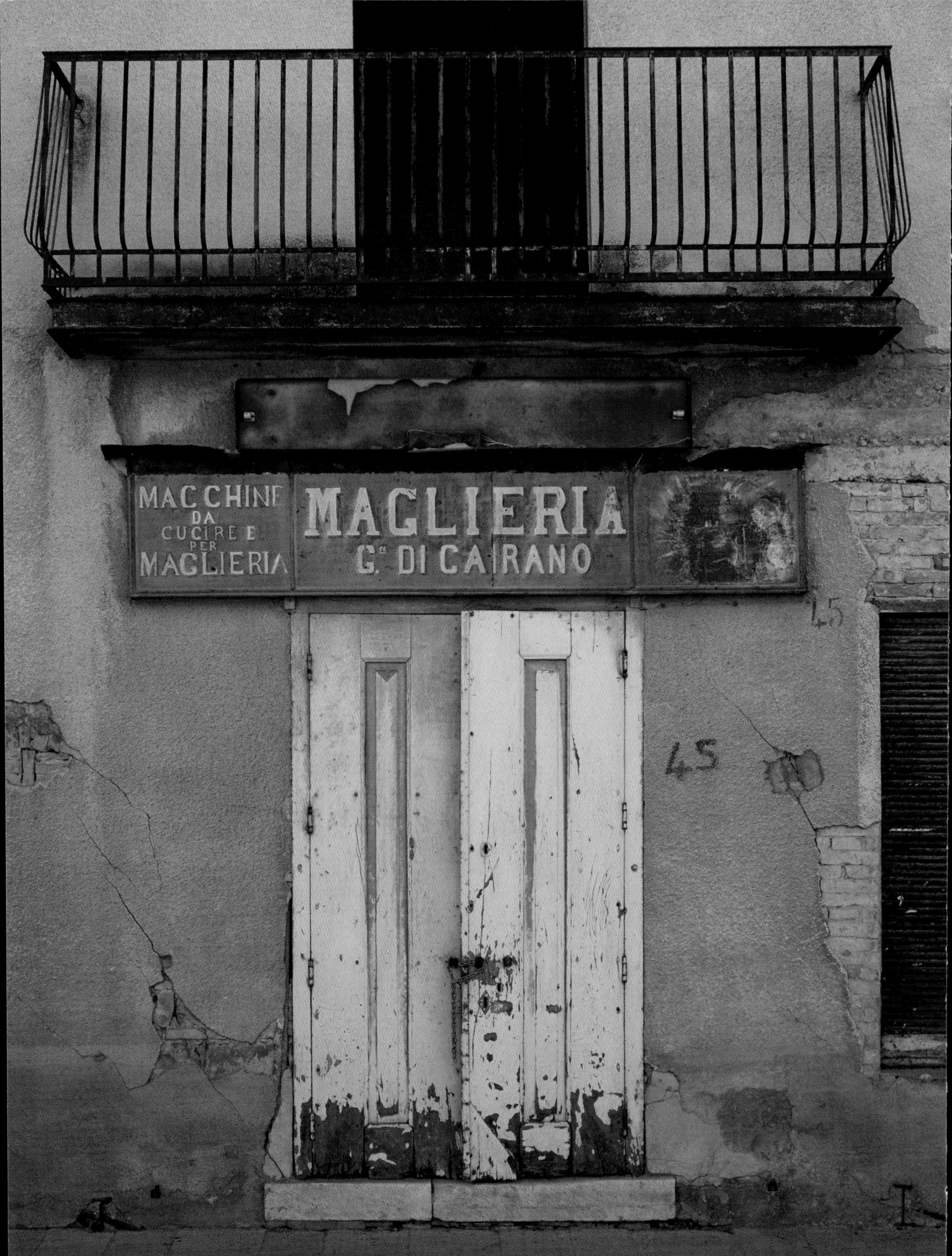

MACCHINE DA CUCIRE E PER MAGLIERIA
MAGLIERIA
G.te DI CAIRANO
45

EGGS WITH PEAS AND TOMATO
UOVA CON PISELLI E POMODORI

Nonna used to make this in England when she came for the winters when I was still at school. It is one of the first things that I learnt to cook, figuring it out from taste memory in my teens. It became a staple when I was a student and there was nothing left in the house. I make it now with the smallest fresh peas at the start of spring. The method is the same for frozen peas, but the cooking of fresh peas is much quicker and the result superior.

FOR 4

1 small red onion, sliced

1 garlic clove, sliced

500g shelled peas, fresh or frozen

4 tbsp Pommarola (page 100) or passata

4 eggs

chilli oil (optional)

sea salt, black pepper and extra virgin olive oil

Sweat the onion in 2 tablespoons of olive oil in a medium saucepan until they are translucent. Add the garlic with a pinch of salt and pepper. When soft and sweet, add the peas, stir and follow with the tomato sauce. Cover with water by 3cm, a lid and simmer for 15 minutes or more.

Remove the lid when the peas have changed colour so that they are all a darker hue and soft but not breaking up. This will take more or less time depending on whether your peas are fresh, very fresh, frozen, big or small, but something like 20 minutes in total.

Add more liquid if the peas are not well covered. Break the eggs into the four corners of the pan, trying to keep them apart – don't stir. Turn down the heat, cover again and cook until the eggs are ready. Serve in bowls with some bread to mop up the juices and a drizzle of dried chilli oil, if you like.

TOMATO FRITTATA RUTHIE ROGERS

FRITTATA AL POMODORO RUTHIE ROGERS

This is straight from the boss, something she makes at home rather than serves in the restaurant. It's evocative for me as we ate this all summer in between shooting her *Classic Italian Cookbook* in southern Tuscany with Rose Gray. It's a dish without a time. Quick to prepare; quick to enjoy; fine to eat standing up but also great to linger over with a glass of wine.

I have tried hard not to be too specific with ingredients but here I must insist that this is made with only the very ripest and tastiest tomatoes at the height of summer and spanking-fresh eggs. This is because it's what Ruthie would insist on when making it for us. It would be less than half the dish otherwise.

Add some cheese if that's your thing but it's not really necessary.

FOR 1

2 eggs

½ ripe oxheart tomato or 1 plum tomato, cut into 2cm slices

2 small basil sprigs

sea salt, black pepper and extra virgin olive oil

Break the eggs into a bowl, season and lightly mix with a fork.

Heat a 25cm trusty pan to smoking hot with oil just covering the bottom. Add the tomato and turn over with a spatula as soon as it is hot, i.e. quite quickly. You don't really want to cook it, just heat up and scorch it a bit.

Add the basil and pour over the eggs, moving them a little after 20 seconds when the middle has started to cook so that that cooked egg is distributed throughout the pan. Position everything to look pretty, if you care about this sort of thing. Cook for 1 minute.

Flip and cook for 1 minute more.

WHITE ASPARAGUS WITH EGG SAUCE
ASPARAGI BIANCHI DEL NORD

This comes from Bassano in the north of Italy, a place famous for distilling and where they grow prized, white asparagus. I have recently discovered that the Wye valley produces the spears closer to home.

FOR 2

3 eggs, as fresh as possible

½ lemon, juiced

1 tablespoon of salted capers, finely chopped

1 gherkin, finely chopped

1 bunch (about 15 spears) white asparagus

black pepper and extra virgin olive oil

Place the eggs in boiling water for 10 minutes, then carefully remove and run under a cold tap until cool enough to peel. Separate the yolks from the whites.

Crush the yolks in a bowl with a fork and add the lemon juice. Add three tablespoons of olive oil in stages, whisking with the fork to make an emulsion. Finely chop the whites, then stir into the yolk emulsion with the capers and gherkins. Taste to check whether it needs a little more salt or lemon juice.

Clean the asparagus. White asparagus needs peeling right from below the tip. If you use a speed peeler, do it at least twice to get through the bitter part. Cook in boiling salted water for 7 minutes. Test the spears are soft enough with the tip of a knife, or better yet, cut the end off one and eat it.

Serve with the sauce and a grind of fresh black pepper.

WILD ASPARAGUS WITH SAUSAGE AND EGG
ASPARAGI E UOVA DEL SUD

There is a trattoria in the south of Italy run by my father's school friend. Whenever she sees him, she makes this. Substitute wild asparagus for sprue or regular asparagus, sliced lengthways.

FOR 2

50g good simple salami, chopped into pieces

1 garlic clove, sliced

1 bunch asparagus, spears snapped at the end and sliced into long thin strips

3 eggs, as fresh as possible

1 tablespoon dried wild oregano

extra virgin olive oil, salt and black pepper

Fry the sausage in 3 tablespoons of oil over a medium heat in a large frying pan. After 1 minute, add the garlic and continue frying until sticky.

Add the asparagus strips, toss and just cover with water. Bring to the boil and continue to cook until they have lost their vivid colour – about 10 minutes – and the pan is dry again.

Whisk the eggs a bit with a fork and season with salt and the oregano. Add them into the pan scrambling with a wooden spoon. After 30 seconds turn the pan off, allowing the eggs to finish cooking in the residual heat.

Serve with black pepper.

FRIED COURGETTE FLOWERS WITH TOMATO

FIORI DI ZUCCA FRITTI AL POMODORO

Perhaps the most popular of all Italian appetisers is zucchini flowers deep-fried in a light batter. I prefer to shallow-fry the flowers in egg and add some freshness with raw tomatoes, or with a light tomato sauce.

FOR 4

20 large male courgette flowers (i.e. without the fruit)

3 very fresh eggs

50g Parmesan or other hard cheese, grated

1–2 ladlefuls fresh tomato sauce (see page 100) or a few very ripe summer tomatoes, sliced – I like both and can't choose which!

10 fresh mint leaves

sea salt, black pepper and extra virgin olive oil

Remove the stamens from the blossoms. You don't have to be too careful – allowing them to tear if you have fingers like mine is easier. In a wide bowl, whisk the eggs well with a fork. Season with the cheese and some salt, then add the flowers. Make sure to turn them over so that they are drenched on all sides.

Heat a non-stick frying pan to a good heat with a couple of tablespoons of oil. Have a large plate with a doubled-up piece of kitchen paper ready. Add the flowers to the hot oil one by one using your fork. Rather than overcrowd the pan, give each a bit of room and cook in batches. After about 30 seconds use tongs or a slotted spoon to turn them over in the order that they were introduced. After another 30 seconds remove them to the plate before cooking the next round.

Layer the flowers on a serving dish interspersing with the tomatoes or sauce. Season and tear over the mint leaves before serving.

SAUCES

I often prefer my meat and fish simply prepared, grilled, roasted or boiled, and I always knock up something tasty to go with it. At its most simple it might just be a grated carrot stirred into mustard with olive oil, parsley and lemon. The following sauces can be used as guidelines, the basis for making a thousand other variations. With a few staple piquant ingredients in the cupboard there is a myriad of options.

CHILLI SAUCE | CREMA DI PEPERONCINI

It probably hasn't escaped your notice that there is a little dried chilli in most of the recipes. I remember Alastair Little writing that you couldn't mix chilli and black pepper, and although I don't actually agree, it must have stayed with me because I normally plump for one or the other.

We always have some type of chilli dressing in the cupboard. The simplest of these is a jar of chopped dried chillies under oil which gets topped up irregularly and must have somewhere in it chillies dating back many years. It looks more like a Chinese chilli sauce, which I also buy from time to time. It gets put on everything and is especially useful for tarting up things that we can also serve to kids and relations. It came in very handy with the boring Christmas turkey. Actually, we must start a new one.

This fresh chilli sauce requires a bit more work, but has a lovely texture and a mellower flavour, well suited to flaky white fish. It doesn't last as well as the chilli oil so make just this amount and use within a few weeks. Spread on toast, with a vegetable or an anchovy nduja-type hit. What I like about this is that the chillies bring everything including acidity, so that no vinegar or anything else is necessary.

FOR 6

10 large fresh chillies, stalks removed and halved lengthways

½ garlic clove

50ml extra virgin olive oil, plus extra to serve

chopped fresh oregano (optional)

sea salt

Use a teaspoon to scrape out the seeds from the chillies, but leave some if you think they aren't hot enough. Beware of burning your hands; wear gloves or touch the chillies as little as possible. Be sure to wash your hands thoroughly after handling them and avoid contact with your eyes.

Heat a large dry frying pan and put the chillies in with a good pinch of salt and toss. Turn the heat to its lowest setting. Keep the chillies in the pan, turning them over from time to time, for 8 minutes. It doesn't matter if they colour a little bit but that is not the objective. The idea is to let them sweat and dry a bit, not totally cook.

Transfer to a blender and buzz with the garlic. Once smooth, add the oil and pulse again. Taste and stir through some oregano, if you like. I often pour a little more oil on top and garnish with a chopped herb so that it looks nice before I serve it.

COOKED SALSA VERDE | SALSA VERDE COTTA

This is a luxurious cooked alternative to your usual salsa verde. Best with vegetables, polenta or plain white fish. Please add a few olives and a pinch of hot chilli if you'd like to.

FOR 4

1 garlic clove, finely chopped

1 tbsp salted capers

4 salted anchovy fillets, roughly chopped

12 sage leaves, chopped

100ml double cream

100g spinach

50g parsley

black pepper and extra virgin olive oil

Heat 3 tablespoons of olive oil in a small pan with the garlic and capers. When they begin to fry, add the anchovies and sage. Add the cream, lower the heat and reduce until thick. Turn off.

Boil the spinach and parsley together for 2 minutes. Run under the tap to cool, squeeze dry and chop well or coarsely blitz. Add to the garlic and cream mixture and season with black pepper.

HORSERADISH SAUCE | SALSA DI RAFANO

For grilled, boiled and roasted meats. This is also good with raw sliced beef. Fresh horseradish is easier to find at the fruit and veg shop than in the supermarket but it lasts very well wrapped in the fridge.

FOR 4

50g breadcrumbs

red wine vinegar

150g horseradish, grated and then chopped

5 mint sprigs, shredded

6 sundried tomatoes, pre-soaked if necessary and chopped

¼ garlic clove, crushed

sea salt, black pepper and extra virgin olive oil

Combine the crumbs with a tablespoon of water and a little flick of vinegar in a small bowl. Add the horseradish, mint, tomatoes and garlic along with salt and pepper to taste, then add 4 tablespoons of oil and thoroughly combine.

GARLIC SAUCE | AGLIATA

Cooking the garlic in milk greatly softens the flavour. This is good with raw sliced vegetables and plenty of black pepper. It also works well with boiled or grilled meats and fish.

FOR 5

250ml whole milk

5 garlic cloves

dash vinegar

75ml extra virgin olive oil

sea salt

Put the milk in a small pan with the garlic and bring to a simmer. Add a pinch of salt and turn down the heat. Allow the garlic to cook for 30 minutes while the milk reduces. The slower the better here.

When there is virtually no milk left and before the pan scorches, transfer the contents to a small food processor or mortar and pestle. Don't worry if it looks a little edgy, it will smooth out later. Add the vinegar.

Turn on the food processor/begin to grind and add the oil, only a little at a time in a stream, as if you were making mayonnaise. It's much easier than mayonnaise to emulsify. Taste for seasoning adding extra vinegar if necessary.

ALMOND AND SAFFRON SAUCE | SALSA DI MANDORLE E ZAFFERANO

This is nice with fish cooked really plainly. It also works well with grilled quail.

FOR 4

2 onions, finely sliced

50g almonds

2 garlic cloves, sliced

8 thyme sprigs, leaves only

1 bay leaf

¼ dried chilli, flaked

1 tbsp wine vinegar

a few saffron threads, soaked in boiling water

10 olives, pitted and chopped

sea salt and extra virgin olive oil

Put 3 tablespoons of olive oil in a small pan and sweat the onions, almonds and garlic with a pinch of salt. Do this slowly over a low heat so that the onions release their sweetness.

Add the thyme leaves, bay leaf, a pinch of chilli and a generous tablespoon of vinegar and turn up the heat. Once that has reduced, add the saffron and water and continue to reduce. When the liquid has mostly evaporated, remove from the heat, add more olive oil and the olives.

PINE NUT SAUCE | SALSA AI PINOLI

This cold sauce has a good quantity of pine nuts and oil for richness. It needs the pepper to act as a counterbalance and, if you crush it freshly as per this recipe, you'll get the maximum aromatic benefit. Great with boiled or roasted meat. It also works well with boiled courgettes.

FOR 6

50g pine nuts

100g good-quality bread, sliced

75ml milk

¼ garlic clove

dash of vinegar

100ml extra virgin olive oil, plus extra for toasting the nuts

25g grated Parmesan

sea salt and 10 black peppercorns

Preheat the oven to 170°C/fan 150°C/gas 3. Toss the pine nuts with a slick of oil and some salt and toast on a baking tray for 5 minutes.

Soak the bread slices in the milk and an equal amount of water. In a mortar and pestle pound the peppercorns with the garlic and almost all the pine nuts. Once smooth, add the bread, a tiny dash of vinegar and the oil in a slow stream, stirring with the pestle. Add the Parmesan. Taste for seasoning and sprinkle with the rest of the pine nuts.

PARSLEY AND BROTH SAUCE | SALSA DI PREZZEMOLO E BRODO

This is well suited to poached chicken (see page 188). Cook the potato with the bird or other meat and use its stock to finish the sauce.

FOR 4

4 parsley or other soft herb sprigs

1 tsp salted capers

2 salted anchovy fillets

1 egg, hard-boiled

1 medium potato (floury not waxy), boiled

1 tsp wine vinegar

1–2 ladlefuls meat broth

75ml extra virgin olive oil

Turn the parsley to a paste in a mortar and pestle. Add the capers and anchovy and continue to pound. Add the boiled egg yolk and half of the white and then the potato and vinegar. At this point, continuing to mix, add a ladleful of broth and some of the oil. Continue until all the oil is used up, adding more broth to loosen if desired.

Pour the sauce over the poached meat.

RADICCHIO SAUCE | SALSA DI RADICCHIO

This is a simple, bittersweet sauce for serving with fish. It keeps well in the fridge for several days.

FOR 6

1 onion, sliced

1 head radicchio

2 salted anchovy fillets

150ml red wine

1 rosemary sprig

½ lemon

sea salt, black pepper and extra virgin olive oil

Put the onion in a pan with a little olive oil and a sprinkling of salt. Sweat very slowly over the lowest flame until the onion is 100 per cent cooked. It may take 20 minutes or more.

Shred the radicchio, losing only the woodiest part of the stem. Add to the pan along with the anchovy. Once the radicchio looks like it has begun to cook a bit, pour in the wine. Bring to the boil and then reduce over a medium heat.

Pick off the rosemary needles, squeeze over the lemon juice and chop them incredibly finely, rocking your knife over.

Once the pan is almost dry transfer the contents to a food processor. Buzz, adding the rosemary, pepper and then 50ml of your favourite olive oil in a thin stream.

AL FORNO
BAKED GOODS

BAKED GOODS

If I had my time again I think that I might take a sideways step and be a baker. I was put off for the same reason others avoid my profession – the hours. In my early twenties, I did work experience at a family-run bakery in the south of Italy, getting up at what felt like the crack of dawn only to discover that much of the bread was already in the oven and I'd missed the action. Thank goodness I'm not a morning person. Baked goods are my weakness, and my willpower would never stand up to being surrounded by them day in, day out without indulging.

Whenever possible, I always try to look at where the action happens: far behind the counter of the bakery. The sight of the big, planetary mixers and stacks of flour inspire the child within and stir the memory. There, the potential of flour and water seems infinite. As a boy, Nonna would commission me to ferry roasting trays of meat and fish to the town *forno*, with the reward of tearing at hot pieces of still-warm bread or pizza on the way back. Though Nonna had an oven at home, as did most of the townspeople, they used this communal one as a meeting point, lingering to discuss what was on the menu and how it was best cooked. These are some of my most cherished food memories.

When I returned to London in 2001 it was hard to find good bread at work. They bought Poilâne bread and other loaves were flown over from Altamura in Puglia for bruschetta! If I wanted good bread at home, I made the trip across town to St John restaurant in Clerkenwell, which produced excellent sourdough long before the rest of London caught on. Most of my favourite restaurants now bake their own bread using natural yeasts. Even at restaurants regarded as the best in the world, I often find the warm, rustic bread and butter that come first the best bit of the meal.

Two Italian bakeries in particular, though very different in themselves, have inspired the recipes in this chapter. One is in the south of Italy, on the street where my grandmother lived. On a recent trip back to the area, I took my wife to visit the bakery. They wrapped up for us massive triangles of pizza with deliciously squidgy oven-baked tomatoes nestling in the dough; potato pizza scattered with rosemary and garlic; pizza with sweet, sweet onions almost like a pissaladière, but better. Back on the road, our car soon smelt like a tiny mobile bakery and, by the time we reached my parents' in Radicondoli, needless to say the picnic was all gone.

The other bakery that has inspired me is in Liguria, close enough to the seafront to take a cache of oil-blotched paper bags and find a bench to sit on and look out at the water, munching, with the gulls circling wildly overhead. The combination of salty air and salty snacks such as *focaccia di Recco* (see page 240), sandwiching molten cheese, makes me think of the summer and freedom.

VERY BASIC PIZZA DOUGH
IMPASTO PER PIZZA

Letting the dough rise slowly in the fridge improves the end result but does require some forethought. Skip this and go to the second rise somewhere warm for an hour or two if you're in a hurry.

MAKES 2 STANDARD-SIZE BAKING TRAYS

5g fresh yeast

320ml water

250g organic white bread flour

250g organic semola flour or kamut flour

10g sea salt

50ml extra virgin olive oil

To make the dough, mix the yeast with the water in a bowl and leave for 5 minutes. Mix the yeasty water into the flours with the salt. This can be done in a bowl and then transferred to a clean work surface for kneading. Knead for 8 minutes, turning the dough by 90 degrees and stretching it out continually. Once the dough is soft and springy, cover with cling film and allow it to rise for 2 hours until doubled in size. Knock down before moving to the fridge for 24 hours. Allow the dough to come back to room temperature before stretching to use as your pizza base.

TOMATO PIZZA

PIZZA AL POMODORO

This is the pizza that I used to carry to the brick oven as a child. But it is not just for sentimental reasons that it might be my favourite pizza. It is one of the best suited to making at home. It is relatively thick for modern tastes and has soft, almost soggy dough under the tomato, which provides a lovely contrast to the crisp base. Use the most lightweight oven tray possible. Lining a flyaway, non-stick aluminium tray with lard is my top tip.

MAKES 2 STANDARD-SIZE BAKING TRAY PIZZAS

ripe tomatoes, preferably plum or San Marzano

1 quantity Very Basic Pizza Dough (page 215)

flour for dusting

***strutto* (lard) or butter for greasing the trays**

1 tsp dried or 1 tbsp fresh oregano

sea salt and extra virgin olive oil

Cut the tomatoes into segments about 2cm across. Season with salt and oil, and put to one side to marinate.

Preheat the oven to 220°C/fan 200°C/gas 7.

Divide the dough into two on a floured surface. Grease two baking trays generously. Place the first half of the dough onto one of the trays and, using your fingertips, stretch it out towards the edges. It should be soft enough to allow you to do this. If it sticks to your hands, try wetting your fingers first. Be mindful to keep it more or less even, moving your fingers around the dough. If you make a hole it is not a problem. The tray should be full of relatively thick dough. Now repeat with the other tray and piece of dough.

Cover each pizza with the tomatoes, pressing them down into the dough. Top this with the oregano. It is up to you if you would like to add a few pieces more of sea salt to crunch on. I would; my doctor would rather I didn't. Leave covered at room temperature for 15–30 minutes, or longer, if need be, in the fridge.

Bake on the top shelf of the oven for 35 minutes. This relatively long bake will ensure that the pizza is as nice and crisp on the base as it is soft and billowy in the middle. Eat with your fingers right away, remembering to hide a piece that you can have cold for breakfast the next day.

POTATO PIZZA
PIZZA CON PATATE

As a piece of pizza to eat in your fingers while on the go, a slice with potatoes takes some beating. Along with, although not before, *pasta e fagioli*, it is an absolute favourite double-carbohydrate treat. The contrast in the different textures of the two carbs is what makes it toothsome and champion.

MAKES 2 STANDARD-SIZE BAKING TRAY PIZZAS

1 quantity Very Basic Pizza Dough (page 215)

flour for dusting

***strutto* (lard) or butter for greasing the trays**

4 baking potatoes

1 tsp dried or 1 tbsp fresh oregano

sea salt and extra virgin olive oil

Preheat the oven to 220°C/fan 200°C/gas 7.

Divide the dough into two on a floured surface. Grease two baking trays generously. Place the first half of the dough onto one of the trays and, using your fingertips, stretch it out towards the edges. It should be soft enough to allow you to do this. If it sticks to your hands, try wetting your fingers first. Be mindful to keep it more or less even, moving your fingers around the dough. If you make a hole it is not a problem. The tray should be full of relatively thick dough. Now repeat with the other tray and piece of dough.

Chip the potatoes into little shards, whittling with the tip of a sharp knife – think skinny fries. They need to be thin enough to cook in time with the pizza.

Toss them with a few tablespoons of oil and the oregano. Spread them across the pizzas, sprinkling with sea salt.

Bake on the top shelf of the oven for 35 minutes.

RICOTTA STUFFED PIZZA
PIZZA CON RIPIENO DI RICOTTA

This is a new one on me; a recipe passed down by new friends. They make the filling with the same things as the Ravioli in this book (see page 49). It's a simple and excellent idea that I'm going to make for evermore. It's another pizza that really lends itself to a domestic oven.

MAKES 2 STANDARD-SIZE BAKING TRAY PIZZAS

1 quantity Very Basic Pizza Dough (page 215)

small bunch parsley, chopped

500g ricotta

2 eggs

***strutto* (lard) or butter for greasing the trays**

flour for dusting

sea salt, black pepper and extra virgin olive oil

Divide the dough into four pieces. Allow to relax and rise again so they become malleable.

Preheat the oven to 220°C/fan 200°C/gas 7.

Make the filling by mixing the parsley with the ricotta and eggs. Season with salt and pepper.

Grease the oven trays and stretch two of the balls of dough on a floured surface using a rolling pin. Finish by spreading them with your fingers into the two trays. It is good if the dough comes up the sides a bit.

Divide the ricotta mix between the two trays of dough, spreading it out but leaving a gap to seal around the rim. Roll out the remaining pieces of dough and use to cover, crimping the edges. It can be quite rough.

Make a couple of holes through the top by snipping with a pair of scissors. Dribble with olive oil and scatter over some big grains of salt.

Bake for 35 minutes until the base is well cooked.

FRIED PIZZA STUFFED WITH BROCCOLI

PETTOLE AI BROCCOLI

Pettole are traditionally saved for Christmas. Stuffed with a wide variety of things you could legitimately add *nduja*, salt cod or keep them totally plain. It is also nice to make a sweet version by heating a little honey with lemon juice until runny and pouring over.

FOR 4

200g organic white bread flour

50g rye flour

½ sachet fast yeast

5g sea salt

500g broccoli (any type) or cauliflower

2 tablespoons salted capers, rinsed

2 tablespoons olives, pitted and roughly chopped

1 red pepper in vinegar (see page 104), chopped

sea salt and black pepper

sunflower oil

Make a wet dough in the bowl of your mixer with the flat beater. Start with the flours mixed with the yeast and then 200ml of tepid water and the 5g of salt. Change to the dough hook and knead for 10 minutes. Then cover and leave somewhere warm to rise until doubled for about 1½ hours.

In the meantime, chop the broccoli or cauliflower into florets and chunks a few centimetres long. Include the stalks, peeled if thick. Boil in salted water for 4 minutes. Mix with a tablespoon of olive oil and the capers, olives and the pepper while steaming hot.

When cooled, carefully add the broccoli or cauliflower mix into the dough, trying to knock it back as little as possible. Leave to rise again for 30 minutes.

When ready to cook heat a pan filled by no more than a third with the oil until hot. Check if it has come up to temperature by either using a thermometer or place in a small piece of dough to see if it fizzles. Take two spoons and push little balls of the dough into the hot oil and fry for 8 minutes until golden.

Remove with a slotted spoon to a plate lined with kitchen paper to blot any remaining oil. Scatter with a little salt. Eat right away.

FLATBREAD
SCHIACCIATA FIORENTINA

This ultra-thin Tuscan focaccia is a great way to kick-start an appetite. Top with herbs, thin slices of peeled vegetables or seeds before cooking. Float on soups or eat with *salumi*. It is satisfyingly straightforward to make and keeps well.

FOR 4

235ml tepid water

20g fresh yeast

20ml extra virgin olive oil, plus extra for sprinkling

375g organic flour (use a mix if you like), plus extra for dusting

5g sea salt, plus extra for sprinkling (optional)

small fresh red chilli, chopped (optional)

fresh herb leaves – thyme, rosemary etc. (optional)

Put the water into a large bowl. It can be the one on your stand mixer if you'd prefer not to knead by hand. Dissolve the yeast by rubbing in with your fingers. Add the oil and most of the flour. Mix together. When you have a rough dough, add the salt followed by the rest of the flour. Knead for 10 minutes, pounding the dough with your wrist while stretching with your other hand.

If you are doing this in a mixer – I always do – then install the dough hook attachment and knead on the second speed for about 7 minutes. The dough should be stretchy and smoother; how much will depend on your flour.

Turn the dough out onto a clean work surface, cut into four, shape a little, dust with flour and cover with a damp cloth. Leave somewhere warm to rise. This will take about 1½ hours.

Preheat the oven to its highest setting, about 240°C/fan 220°C/gas 9 and line a baking tray with baking paper.

Flour a clean work surface and roll out the dough. Don't press too hard on the rolling pin and keep throwing flour around in thin bursts so that it doesn't clump.

Turn and roll, turn and roll, and so on until you have a piece of dough only a few millimetres thick. The shape doesn't matter as long as it fits your baking tray. Spread the dough out on the lined tray and flick on some extra oil. I like to add big salt crystals for crunch and hot red pepper, but you can embellish with herbs if you like. Repeat with the other three pieces of dough.

Open the oven for the briefest time possible to put in the baking trays and slam shut. Bake for 5 minutes or until golden and bubbled. Eat as soon as it is cool enough to break into pieces with your hands.

POLENTA | GRANOTURCO

One of my father's older sisters lives in Bergamo in northern Italy near the Alps. It is well known that, in Italy, food varies vastly from region to region and that in the north they favour richer, more substantial ingredients and cooking. In my aunt's home, a polenta cooker is always turning, as de rigueur as a rice cooker in Asia or an electric kettle and toaster here. If I liken the polenta cooker to a copper tabletop cement mixer, I'm not sure it is going to endear polenta to you. What it teaches us is that polenta must be stirred regularly and cooked for a long time. My aunt cooks it in a mix of 50/50 milk and water for ages. She puts the polenta on to cook well ahead of knowing what's for lunch as, for her, it is a staple of any lunch.

One holiday, Mum and Dad decided to buy a polenta cooker to take home with us. I remember them exclaiming that finally we too would have nice polenta. Another lesson here. Polenta is only really good when it has been recently milled. Stale polenta is no better than stale flour, or pulses, or tea or coffee for that matter. And when I was growing up in England the only polenta you could find was below par. The good stuff – the stuff you could always find in Italy, and which you can increasingly hunt down here – is made from excellent corn, dried on the cob and milled. It has a strong, maize aroma. Just like the best pasta, it should be good enough to eat on its own; oil and Parmesan would be a bonus. Now when I buy, I employ the same tactic as I use with dried beans and other dry goods: I look for packets with a long expiry date suggesting that they have been harvested and milled recently.

I used to be put off cooking polenta at home because of the washing-up. Now I make sure to cook in a pan that can be scoured after. If you cook on just the right heat, a hard, taco-like skin forms on the bottom of the pan – like the crust on the base of a paella pan – which, with a little serious coaxing, can be a tasty cook's snack. My dear colleague Claudio does a good line in crisped polenta topped with chilli and cheese.

Cooking in a mix of water and milk, following my aunt's method, is a good way to bring out the gentle character of polenta. For every 200g, bring a litre of water or a mix of water and milk to the boil in your heaviest pan with a pinch of salt. Add the polenta in a stream with one hand while whisking with the other to prevent any lumps from forming. Be careful as it returns to the boil because it is scalding hot – like lava. Once bubbling, turn down the heat to a very minimum. Use a heat diffuser if your hob doesn't go low. Cook for up to 2 hours, covered with a lid, and stir from time to time. When ready, it will have more of a tendency to come away from the sides of the pan.

If you make it like this then you can flavour it with butter, cheese, oil or vegetable purée. Sometimes I add vegetables to the cooking polenta so that they dissolve, leaving only their sweetness: pumpkin, leeks and onions are among my favourites. If you pour it out onto a cool, clean surface – this was once done simply over a table for people to slice there and then – it will set so that you can cut it into slices to griddle, roast or fry. Coat with oil and chopped herbs and roast or fry into Neapolitan street food and eat with sausages or onions.

When my wife and I were in Abruzzo on holiday it was truffle season, and chalkboards outside cafés announced polenta with fresh truffle sauce for a few euros. Old men sat at their cauldrons stirring the maize meal and muttering to their fellows like incantations. When we ordered, rough ladles were spread over paper plates and truffles grated generously over the buttery, yellow mountains. It exemplified everything that is good about polenta, humble food that with little interference can be made into a meal fit for a king.

BAKED POLENTA

POLENTA AL FORNO

You could be clever and make use of leftover polenta here. This recipe calls for 500g cooled cooked polenta. I enjoy these for breakfast also, omitting the cabbage leaves and cooking on the hob like a polenta hotcake, turning them after five minutes.

FOR 8

200g coarse polenta or cornmeal

10g salt

1 sachet active yeast

200g '00' flour

8 large outside leaves of a cabbage, washed and dried

sage leaves/anchovy fillets/sausage meat/pecorino/herbs of your preference (all optional)

extra virgin olive oil

Make the polenta well ahead. Bring 600ml water to the boil in a heavy-based pan. Scatter in the polenta as you whisk to avoid grummi – lumps – and then simmer until cooked according to the packet instructions. Turn out onto a plate and allow to cool and set.

Once you are ready to begin, break pieces of the polenta into the bowl of a stand mixer. Begin to beat it with the flat beater until smooth. Add 50ml of warm water, salt and 2 tablespoons of oil and continue beating. Lower the speed and mix in the flour with the yeast. Cover the bowl with cligfilm and leave somewhere warm to rise until doubled in size, about 2 hours, or overnight in the fridge.

Preheat the oven to 240°C/fan 220°C/gas 9.

Take the cabbage leaves and put a spoonful of the polenta dough square in the middle of the leaf. Place over a sage leaf and a piece of salted anchovy, or alternatively some sausage meat, or a piece of pecorino cheese, or herbs of your choice and drizzle with oil. Roughly twist the edges of the paper up into a parcel so that it will steam. When several are ready, place them on a baking tray towards the top of the hot oven.

Bake for 15 minutes.

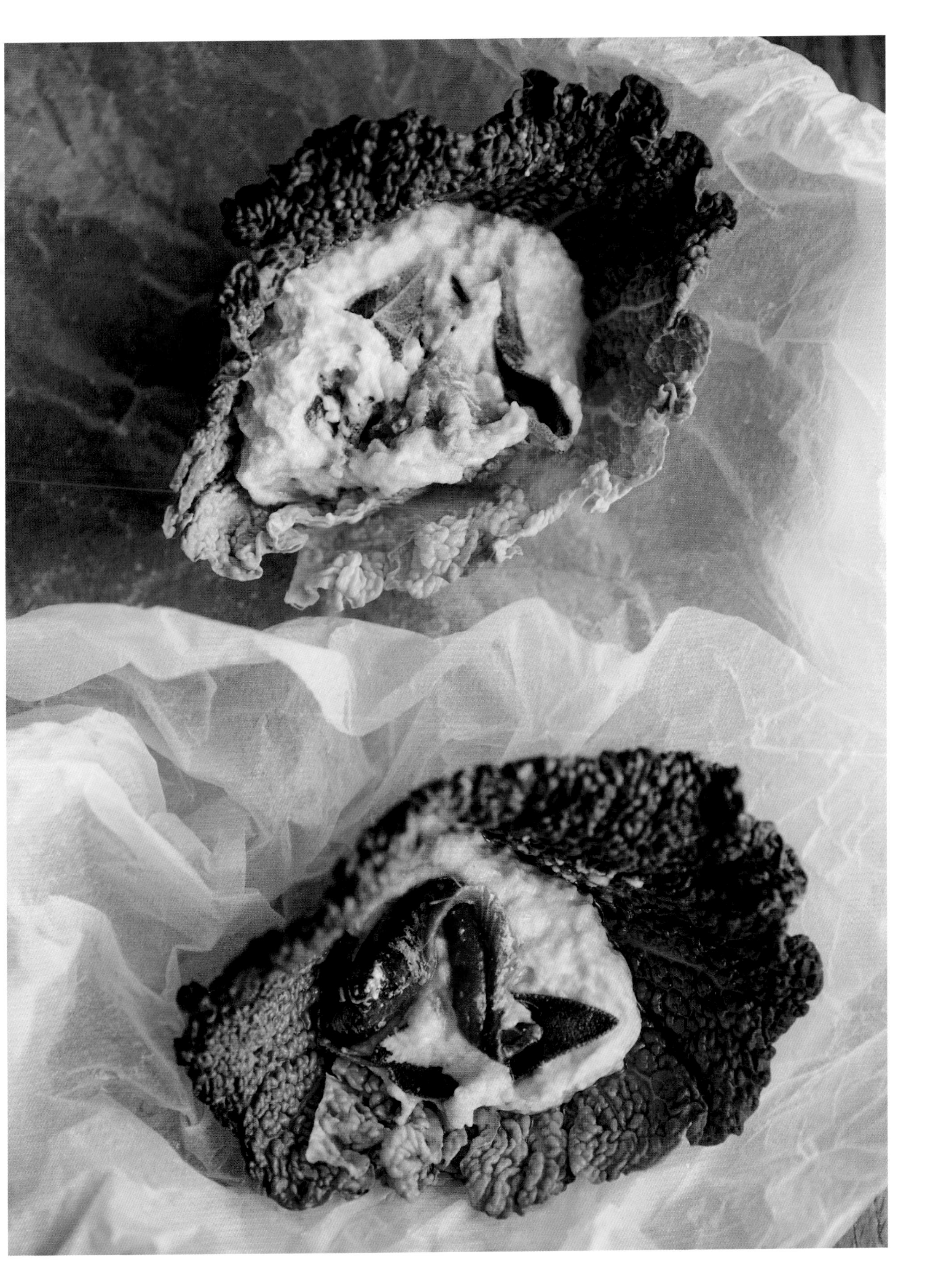

POLENTA BREAD
MIGLIACCIO

When Nonna first taught me how to make this, she said they used to eat it when there was no bread. I think that traditionally *ciccioli*, the leftover fried pieces of pork from rendering lard, would have been used, but we made it with pancetta and she insisted that even a little salami would have been good.

FOR 2

butter or lard for greasing

60g lardo or pancetta or sausage, cubed

250g pumpkin, peeled and diced

10g sage leaves

4 slices onion

¼ dried chilli, crushed

200g coarse polenta or cornmeal

100g scamorza, chopped into 2cm pieces

sea salt and extra virgin olive oil

Preheat the oven to 200°C/fan 180°C/gas 6 and butter a trusty small (20cm-ish) heavy-based ovenproof dish or baking tin.

Put 2 tablespoons of oil in a pan and fry the lardo or equivalent until crispy and melted. Next add the pumpkin and stir. Add the sage, onion and chilli, followed by the polenta. Stir vigorously. It will be very thick. Top up with 200ml water and bring to the boil. Add a good pinch of salt, stir and allow to cook for 5 minutes only. Stir in the cheese.

Pour the mixture into the greased dish. Use a palette knife or spatula to smooth over the top and bake for 50 minutes. The top will be golden and the polenta pulling away from the sides of the dish.

ONION, OLIVE AND CHICKPEA BAKE

FOCACCIA DI CECI, CIPOLLE E OLIVE

This is a halfway house between chickpea *farinata* and Pugliese focaccia. A balance between sweet and substantial, it is incredibly cheap to make and, yes, gluten free. Perfect with a slice of salami and a beer.

FOR 4

300ml water

400g chickpea flour

2 onions, sliced

1 tbsp salted capers

100g small black olives, pitted

1 tbsp dried oregano

100g passata or Pommarola (page 100)

sea salt, black pepper and extra virgin olive oil

Put the water in a bowl and sift in the chickpea flour. Whisk with 10g salt and 10ml oil. Skim off any foam with a ladle, cover and leave to rest somewhere warm for an hour or two. It won't look transformed, but will have improved.

Sweat the onions in 3 tablespoons of olive oil. Once they have begun to soften, season, turn down the heat and cover. Cook slowly for 20 minutes. Add the capers, olives, oregano and passata and continue to cook for another 10 minutes.

Preheat the oven to 210°C/fan 190°C/gas 5 and oil a 30cm non-stick baking tin or an ovenproof dish lined with baking paper.

Pour in the chickpea batter and dot in the onion and olive mixture. Drizzle over 2 tablespoons of oil and bake for 15–20 minutes until unified and golden.

FENNEL SEED AND OLIVE OIL TARALLI

TARALLI AL SEMI DI FINOCCHIO

These little dry aniseed biscuits are eaten with *aperitivo*. They are very moreish with their salty crunch.

MAKES AROUND 30

250g organic white flour

250g organic semola flour

10g fine sea salt

70ml extra virgin olive oil

1 heaped tbsp fennel seeds

200ml white wine

In a large mixing bowl combine the flours with the salt and olive oil and begin to mix using a wooden spoon. Then add the fennel seeds and wine. Mix until you have a dough that you can transfer to a clean work surface for kneading.

Knead for about 10 minutes, turning the dough as you do so, until it is smooth and elastic. Divide into 10 pieces. Take each one and roll out with the palms of your hands to a sausage of about 1cm in diameter. Cut each sausage into three 15cm lengths. Loop them round, making a point with the two ends that you squeeze together.

Bring a large pan of water to the boil and line a tray with a clean towel. Boil the taralli a handful at a time. As soon as the taralli rise to the surface transfer them to the tray. Repeat until all are cooked.

Preheat the oven to 180°C/fan 160°C/gas 4.

Allow the taralli to dry completely before baking for 30 minutes. They will keep for a very long time if stored in a sealed container.

ALMOND AND BLACK PEPPER TARALLI

TARALLI CON MANDORLE E PEPE

This is the classic Neapolitan snack designed to stoke your thirst and keep you nibbling and sipping long into the evening. I find it easier to make without the use of the mixer.

MAKES 20

FOR THE SPONGE

360g organic '00' flour

8g fresh yeast or equivalent dried

120g suet

5g fine sea salt

5g coarsely ground black pepper

150g almonds with skins on, two-thirds roughly blitzed

Make a sponge by thoroughly mixing 80g of the flour with the yeast and 80ml of tepid water. Cover and leave somewhere warm for 2 hours until doubled in size.

Put the suet, salt and flour and in a large bowl and work with your fingertips until it resembles breadcrumbs. Add the chopped almonds and sponge mixture, and then add 100ml of tepid water, mixing until it just comes together as a dough. Do not be tempted to overwork or knead. Cover, and leave to rest for an hour somewhere warm.

Preheat the oven to 200°C/fan 180°C/gas 6 and line a baking tray with baking paper.

Heavily flour the worktop and your hands before taking the dough and uniformly pressing it flat. Keep pressing by hand or gently with a rolling pin to achieve a flat square of dough about 30 x 30 x 1cm. Use a knife to cut into 20 slices 1cm wide. Fold them in half and then use a little water to help them stick. Twist them up two at a time and then pinch the ends together to make a ring.

Place them on the baking tray and decorate with the remaining almonds. Bake for 15 minutes then turn the oven down to 150°C/fan 130°C/gas 2 and continue baking for another 30 minutes.

These, unlike the previous taralli, are most delicious eaten warm.

LIGURIAN BAKERY | LIGURIA AL FORNO

The following recipes use a simple dough that I discovered in Liguria.

There are in fact several ways to make this dough, and this is the first I was shown. It uses milk instead of eggs or oil and is smooth like satin. If you are new to this technique, make double the recipe so you have a bit of spare to get the knack. The dough is rolled extremely thin so takes a bit of practice to use confidently. It should be quite a bit softer than pasta dough, though it can be rolled on a pasta machine and stuffed like ravioli with cheese then deep-fried to become panzerotti.

FOCACCIA FROM RECCO

FOCACCIA DI RECCO

Recco is a town on the Ligurian coast between Genova and Portofino. If you go there you can eat this on the street or at a *focacceria*, where it is treated more like a pizza. If you'd like to make a large one, it's easier to do it with another pair of hands, stretching the dough very gently between you. The stretching of this dough requires a lightness of touch and a minimum of pulling.

If you've never had this before I think you should opt for the plain version, but you can also 'pizzerise' with a tomato and herb topping and a little oil before baking, if you like.

FOR 2

250g organic '00' flour

125ml whole milk

200g stracchino or crescenza cheese

sea salt and extra virgin olive oil

Mix the flour and milk together until you have a dough, then transfer to a clean work surface for kneading. Lightly flour the bench if the dough is tacky. Knead it constantly, rotating all the while, and flouring the worktop where necessary, for about 4 minutes, or longer if your batch is bigger. It will quickly feel very smooth on the outside and will bounce back when pressed with your fingertip.

When smooth to the touch, cover well and leave to rest for at least 30 minutes.

Preheat the oven to 220°C/200°C/gas 7 and oil a light, large non-stick baking tray.

Cut the dough into two roughly equal amounts, but make one slightly bigger than the other. Use the bigger one for the base. Roll it out into a rectangle as thinly as possible, to about 2mm. Keep the tray you are going to use beside you to help you gauge the size and begin to work with your hands. The aim is to make something thinner than regular pasta, almost as thin as filo. The under sheet can be slightly thicker than the top but make sure that it doesn't have any holes in it. The second will have holes made in it, so it's not as much of a problem.

Work with your hands together as if you were praying but with the dough sheet draped over. Carefully move your hands apart, but do this very gently, almost as though trying not to stretch the dough. It will, however, do so. Hop the dough on your hands so that it turns

around by 45 degrees at first and repeat. Pay particular attention to the edges of the dough, not the centre, which will naturally be pulled by the weight of the dough. Stretch the parts that are thicker and avoid those that look too thin.

When large enough to fit, place on the baking tray and dot with pieces of stracchino cheese. Stretch out a second piece of dough, ideally slightly thinner. Place on top of the cheese and cut around the edges with a knife. Crimp the border together and tear a few holes in the top. Lightly sprinkle with olive oil and salt before baking.

Bake for 8 minutes until golden and slightly bubbling through the holes. Eat immediately and make another straight away.

RICE AND HERBS PIE

TORTA SALATA DI RISO E VERDURE

I'm not sure how this compares to the classic recipe but this is the most traditional of 'pies' here.

FOR 4

FOR THE DOUGH

250g organic '0' or '00' flour

125ml whole milk

FOR THE FILLING

200g risotto rice

600ml milk

400ml water

1 small red onion, sliced

2 leeks, sliced

3 eggs

100g Parmesan, grated

nutmeg

2 tbsp marjoram, chopped

1 tbsp rosemary, chopped

3 tbsp fennel seeds, crushed

1 tbsp fresh oregano, chopped

4 anchovy fillets (optional)

sea salt, black pepper and extra virgin olive oil

Make the dough with the flour and milk as per Focaccia di Recco (see page 240). Once made, split into two balls, one slightly larger than the other. Rest for at least 30 minutes.

To make the filling, boil the rice in the milk and water for 10 minutes until cooked. It should remain al dente. Put 2 tablespoons of olive oil in a pan and sweat the onion and leeks with a pinch of salt.

In a large bowl whisk the eggs with the Parmesan and a scratch of nutmeg. Season and taste.

When the onion and leeks are soft, add the herbs to the pan along with the anchovy fillets, if using. Once the anchovies have dissolved, add to the bowl with the eggs and Parmesan and mix in the cooked rice.

Preheat the oven to 210°C/190°C/gas 5. Oil a cake tin or thin flan dish with raised sides large enough to fit all the filling, about 25cm in diameter.

Roll the bigger piece of dough into a thin round large enough to come some way up the sides of the tin. You can use your hands to do this but keep the dough as thin as a sheet of pasta – not thinner. Use it to line the tin and then add the filling. Roll out the second piece of dough in the same way as the first. Place over the top of the filling. Cut around the edges of the dough, then crimp the under layer over the top to seal the border.

Cut little holes in the top with scissors or a knife, sprinkle with olive oil and bake for 30 minutes until steaming and golden on the top. Allow to cool a little before serving.

POTATO AND PORCINI PIE

TORTA SALATA PATATE E FUNGHI

My friend Stevie and I included this in the menu for a supper club we cooked many years ago. An attendee still asks me for the recipe to this day, so here it is.

FOR 4

250g organic '00' flour

125ml whole milk, plus extra for brushing

200g new potatoes, peeled and diced

1 garlic clove, chopped

4 thyme sprigs, leaves only

400g fresh porcini or ceps, cleaned and diced

4 parsley sprigs, leaves only

3 eggs

150ml double cream

75g mature pecorino

sea salt, black pepper and extra virgin olive oil

Make the dough with the flour and milk as per Focaccia di Recco (see page 240). Rest for at least 30 minutes.

Boil the potatoes in salted water for 15 minutes.

Heat 2 tablespoons of olive oil in a pan over a medium heat and add the garlic immediately followed by the thyme, mushrooms and half the parsley. Season and sauté for 5 minutes. If the mushrooms are the dry type, they may need a touch of water; they can be quite loose for this dish.

Whisk the eggs with the cream and add the rest of the parsley, the potatoes, cheese and mushrooms.

Preheat the oven to 210°C/fan 190°C/gas 5. Oil a cake tin or thin flan dish 25cm in diameter with raised sides large enough to fit all the filling.

Roll the dough into a thin round large enough to come some way up the sides of the tin. You can use your hands to do this but keep the dough as thin as a sheet of pasta – not thinner. Use it to line the tin and then add the filling. Turn the edges in on themselves around the top of the pie, removing any excess dough and arranging the border to look nice.

Brush the dough edges with milk and sprinkle with oil. Bake for 30 minutes until golden and set.

AUBERGINE PIE

TORTA SALATA ALLE MELANZANE

This is the one to make in the summer.

FOR 4

250g organic '0' or '00' flour

125ml whole milk, plus extra for brushing

2 aubergines

½ garlic clove, crushed

2 eggs

350g ricotta

bunch basil, leaves only

2 bunches courgette flowers, torn with stamens removed (optional)

sea salt and extra virgin olive oil

Make the dough with the flour and milk as per Focaccia di Recco (see page 240). Rest for at least 30 minutes.

Preheat the oven to 210°C/fan 180°C/gas 5.

Pierce the aubergines several times and bake in the oven for 20 minutes until soft. When cool enough to handle, cut open and scoop out the flesh with a spoon, keeping in long strands if possible.

Place the garlic, a pinch of salt, the eggs and ricotta in a bowl. Whisk together. Add the aubergine flesh, basil and courgette flowers, if using. Season and mix.

Oil a cake tin or thin flan dish with raised sides large enough to fit all the filling, about 25cm in diameter.

Roll the dough into a thin round large enough to come some way up the sides of the tin. You can use your hands to do this but keep the dough as thin as a sheet of pasta – not thinner. Use it to line the tin and then fill with the aubergine stuffing. Turn the edges in on themselves around the top of the pie, removing any excess dough and arranging the border to look nice.

Brush the dough edges with milk and sprinkle with oil. Bake for 25 minutes until set.

SWEET
DOLCE

31
SQUIZY
SLIME BALLS

SWEET

I adore making puddings. The process itself is a treat as, usually, it means I have the time and space to give it my full attention. Tinkering around in the kitchen then is as pleasurable for me as sharing what I've made later on. I would happily wait for these peaceful moments to enjoy making a sweet, were it not for my wife. For the love of her, I find myself scraping around after the vegetables have been eaten, and the plates wiped clean with bread crusts, trying to rustle something up. I've even found myself attempting to caramelise bits of leftover cereal for an impromptu banana split. Having a back-up of little sweet treats in the cupboard could come in very useful.

This chapter is therefore devoted to recipes for filling the biscuit or cake tin and having standbys in the cupboard or freezer, 'in case of emergencies'. Some are worthier than others, but nothing is off-limits. A lot of them are things that you might eat during the day, perhaps to accompany coffees and little drinks, the way that cigarettes used to in the days of my youth.

In Italy, pudding is just less important than in the UK. Guests often bring pastries for after dinner; but even then, they often aren't consumed until a more appropriate time in the mid-afternoon. My favourite dessert would always involve a walk to a patisserie, bar or ice-cream shop where each person could choose their own.

ICE CREAM | GELATO

Ice cream is just the best. I know you agree with me. It is unrivalled, the pinnacle in the pudding stakes. One dear friend, equally besotted, once made the mistake of opening the ice-cream churner at work to pinch a spoonful before the batch was done and the whole lot poured onto the floor. This makes me laugh every time I think of it.

When people are coming to supper my thoughts turn to ice cream. I keep a cheap ice-cream churner permanently in the freezer, just in case. With it, I can make only one flavour at a time. The idea is that any flavour can stand alone, or stand up to a complementary fruit or biscuit accompaniment.

The ice cream in these recipes is different from the *crème anglaise* version. I have employed a few different techniques, but they are all perfectly good for making at home. The quality is natural and is best enjoyed the day it is churned. The methods are straightforward and you may even have most of the ingredients in your kitchen already, just to make something spontaneously.

You can make almost any ice cream without a machine, but I do advise you to get one. You can find them for the same price as this book. I am lucky in that I have enough space in my freezer to keep one permanently on standby, as I recommend you do. If you do go and buy one on the strength of this, and make ice cream for the first time to test it out, try this: purée two cans of stoned lychees with a squeeze of lemon and half the syrup they come with. Churn. Once you see how delicious and easy this sorbet is, you'll be hooked.

If you opt for making ice creams by hand, put a stainless-steel bowl in the freezer before you start. Once the mixture is ready to freeze, place it in the chilled bowl for 45 minutes. Remove and whisk with a fork, then return to the freezer and whisk again after another 30 minutes. Continue doing this for a period of at least 4 hours to break up the ice crystals as much as possible. Then leave for 2 hours, or until you can scoop the ice cream into bowls. It's kind of hard work and, with the exception of a granita, which has a different nature, I'm not sure it's worth it.

Ice cream eaten out, even if supper is at home, is the best dessert. It is impossible to be too full for ice cream. These ice creams are very homemade, deliberately. There is no point in replicating the ice cream from a professional source; rather, they should epitomise the homespun.

APPLE AND LEMON SORBET

SORBETTO DI MELA E LIMONE

This is particularly nice with apples that have some red about them. When cooked they are soft and resemble peaches more than apples. Use an organic unwaxed lemon as you are going to cook it with the skin on.

FOR 6

6 apples

150g caster sugar

1 lemon

200ml water

Don't peel the apples but do wash them, then cut into quarters and remove the core. Wash and cut the lemon into 8 pieces, removing any pips as you go.

Put everything into a pan and bring to the boil. Simmer for 30 minutes until the apples are completely soft. Make sure to keep the lemon pieces under the liquid to help the skin soften.

First put the lemon pieces into a food processor and blitz, then add the rest of the contents of the pan and purée some more. This is to ensure that it's as smooth as possible.

Set aside and, once cool, chill completely in the fridge.

Churn in an ice-cream machine according to the manufacturer's instructions but probably for about 30 minutes. Transfer to the freezer and freeze for 2 hours or until scoopable.

The sorbet is best eaten the same day but it will keep for a week in the freezer. Remove 10 minutes ahead of serving if frozen solid.

C.A.S.T.
281260 - ALMERIA

PUMPKIN SEED ICE CREAM

GELATO AI SEMI DI ZUCCA

This interesting green ice cream is luscious and thick.

FOR 6

1 vanilla pod

700ml whole milk

100g caster sugar

45g cornflour

200g pumpkin seeds

pinch sea salt

6 tablespoons extra virgin olive oil

Split the vanilla pod and add to the milk in a pan, scraping out the seeds. Add half of the sugar. Whisk a ladleful of this mixture into the cornflour, being careful to avoid any lumps. Warm the rest of the vanilla-milk and, when it is hot, whisk in the cornflour concoction and cook until thick, stirring constantly. This will take 4–5 minutes. Do not let the milk boil. Remove from the heat and allow to cool.

In a heavy-based pan, toast the pumpkin seeds over a low flame. Turn them from time to time as they pop. Once they have a pleasant nutty aroma, after about 2 minutes, transfer them to a food processor with the remaining sugar and the salt. Blitz. Once they are well on the way add the oil, preferably with the machine still running, then 3 tablespoons of hot water. This will produce a thick paste.

Add the pumpkin seed paste to the thickened milk. Chill until completely cold, preferably overnight, and churn in an ice-cream machine according to the manufacturer's instructions.

Best eaten as soon as it's scoopable, after about 1–2 hours in the freezer, but this ice cream will keep for a week. Remove from the freezer well ahead of serving to soften once frozen solid.

VICKY PLUM GRANITA

GRANITA ALLE PRUGNE

When you have good fruit, the temptation is to eat it as is. But sweet plums do sing alongside the rasp of a glass of grappa and it inspired a marriage in the form of this granita. This recipe doesn't require an ice-cream machine unless you want a smoother sorbet texture.

FOR 6

1kg very ripe Victoria plums

50g caster sugar, plus extra (optional)

tiny pinch sea salt

50ml grappa, schnapps or eau de vie

lemon juice (optional)

Wash, halve and stone the fruit.

Heat the plums with the sugar and the salt. Once the sugar has dissolved, cook, stirring continually, over a high heat for 20 minutes until the colour has intensified and the liquid somewhat reduced.

Purée and pass through a sieve, removing the skins as you do. Add the alcohol and taste. It should be sweet, but there should be a balance between the power of the alcohol and the tartness of the fruit. Add more sugar and/or lemon if needed.

Refrigerate before freezing in an airtight container. After 50 minutes, remove from the freezer and agitate with a fork. Return and repeat this every 30 minutes for several hours until the characteristically flaky granita texture is achieved.

Alternatively, churn in an ice-cream machine according to the manufacturer's instructions for a smoother sorbet.

Eat within a few days, removing from the freezer 10 minutes ahead of serving to soften.

CHOCOLATE AND COFFEE ICE CREAM

GELATO DI CAFFÈ E CIOCCOLATO

This is a smooth ice cream that is made without an ice-cream machine. Especially useful when in need of ice cream away from home.

FOR 4

95g caster sugar

20g cocoa powder

50g dark chocolate, broken into pieces

2 egg yolks

2 espresso shots (50ml or less)

300ml double cream

tiny pinch sea salt

Slowly heat 100ml of water with 20g of the sugar and the cocoa. Simmer over a moderate heat for 2 minutes, stirring. Remove from the heat and, when slightly cooled, about a minute later, add the chocolate. Stir to melt.

Bring a pan half-full of water to the boil. In a bowl that will fit on top of the pan whisk the egg yolks with the remaining sugar until pale. Place the bowl over the simmering pan and whisk in the coffee. Whisk continually until thick and airy, with a texture like zabaglione but not at all scrambled. This takes about 2 minutes.

Remove the bowl from the heat but continue to whisk while it cools for another minute. Then whisk in the chocolate. Chill either in the fridge or over ice.

Whisk the cream with the salt until it's as thick as the chocolate. Carefully fold the two together using a spatula. Cover and freeze.

Best eaten as soon as it's scoopable, after about 4 hours in the freezer, this ice cream will keep for a week. Remove from the freezer well ahead of serving to soften once frozen solid.

FLOWER OF THE MILK

FIOR DI LATTE

Despite the name, this is all about the cream. I make this when I've got tasty unpasteurised cream. It also works well with crème fraîche. Add vanilla if you like but don't overlook its purity without. You will notice the cornflour less than you would eggs, it's the Sicilian way.

FOR 6

400ml whole milk

45g cornflour

100g caster sugar

tiny pinch sea salt

300ml double cream

Whisk a ladleful of the milk into the cornflour, being careful not to make any lumps. Then heat the rest of the milk in a pan with the sugar and salt to hot but not boiling before whisking in the cornflour mixture. Cook, stirring continuously, over a medium-low heat for 4–5 minutes until thickened. Do not let it boil. Remove from the heat and allow to cool. Stir through the cream and chill completely, preferably overnight.

Churn in an ice-cream machine according to the manufacturer's instructions, but for about 30 minutes. Best eaten as soon as it's scoopable, after about 1–2 hours in the freezer, although this ice cream will keep for a week. Remove from the freezer well ahead of serving to soften once frozen solid.

PINE NUT ICE CREAM
GELATO DI PINOLI

This is an extravagant amount of pine nuts but it's worth it for the amazing flavour. I wouldn't attempt to churn this without a machine.

FOR 4

120g pine nuts

100g caster sugar

2 egg yolks

200ml double cream

200ml whole milk, plus 1–2 tbsp extra

pinch sea salt

In a food processor, or using a mortar and pestle, make a paste with 90g of the pine nuts and half the sugar, adding a tablespoon or two of milk once under way to help render everything creamy.

In a bowl, place the egg yolks with the rest of the sugar and a tiny pinch of salt. Whisk until super-pale and thick, then whisk in the pine nut paste followed by the cream and milk. Leave in the fridge to cool and thicken – overnight is best.

If you like, you can toast the remaining pine nuts for extra crunch. Simply preheat the oven to 170°C/fan 150°C/gas 3 and gently toast with 2 teaspoons of sugar and a teaspoon of milk. This takes around 20 minutes. Allow to cool.

Remove the creamy pine nut mix from the fridge and churn in an ice-cream machine according to the manufacturer's instructions, taking care not to split it as it has a high quantity of cream. Add the remaining nuts, toasted or raw, towards the end of churning so that they remain whole.

Best eaten as soon as it's scoopable, after about 1–2 hours in the freezer, but this ice cream will keep for a week. Remove from the freezer well ahead of serving to soften once frozen solid.

STRAWBERRY ICE CREAM

GELATO DI FRAGOLE

Strawberry ice cream is my daughter's favourite. This recipe has been subjected to the most rigorous testing.

FOR 6

600g strawberries, hulled and halved

50g caster sugar

200ml whole milk

30g cornflour

150ml double cream

70g brown sugar

tiny pinch sea salt

Toss the strawberries in a bowl with the caster sugar. Cover and leave to macerate for at least an hour.

Whisk a ladleful of the milk into the cornflour, being careful not to make any lumps. Then heat the rest of the milk in a pan with the cream, brown sugar and salt. When hot but not boiling, whisk in the cornflour mixture. Cook, stirring continuously, over a medium-low heat for 4–5 minutes until thickened. Do not let it boil. Remove from the heat and allow to cool down completely.

Puree the strawberries in a food processor and, once smooth, add the cooled ice-cream base. Ensure the mixture is completely chilled in the fridge, preferably overnight, before churning in an ice-cream machine according to the manufacturer's instructions.

Best eaten as soon as it's scoopable, after about 1–2 hours in the freezer, but this ice cream will keep for a week. Remove from the freezer well ahead of serving to soften once frozen solid.

PEACH ICE CREAM
GELATO ALLE PESCHE

What is there better than a fresh peach? Peach ice cream.

FOR 6

350ml whole milk
30g cornflour
120g caster sugar
tiny pinch sea salt
700g peaches
½ lemon (optional)

Whisk a ladleful of the milk into the cornflour, being careful not to make any lumps. Then heat the rest of the milk in a pan with 70g of the sugar and the salt. When hot but not boiling, whisk in the cornflour mixture. Cook, stirring continuously, over a medium-low heat for 4–5 minutes until thickened. Do not let it boil. Remove from the heat, allow to cool down and then chill in the fridge, preferably overnight.

In the meantime, segment, stone and cook the peaches with the rest of the sugar in 100ml water. Whizz in a food processor, adding a squeeze of lemon to taste for added tartness if necessary. Stir into the ice-cream base.

Churn in an ice-cream machine according to the manufacturer's instructions. Best eaten as soon as it's scoopable, after about 1–2 hours in the freezer, but this ice cream will keep for a week. Remove from the freezer well ahead of serving to soften once frozen solid.

RICE ICE CREAM
GELATO DI RISO

I started out wanting to make an ice cream that was based around the Scandinavian dessert *riskrem*, a chilled creamy rice pudding that my wife's family traditionally eat on Christmas Eve. I ended up making something that reminds me more of pannacotta.

FOR 6

100g risotto rice
1.2 litres whole milk
1 unwaxed lemon, pared
tiny pinch sea salt
1 vanilla pod, split
150g caster sugar
200ml double cream

Put the rice and milk in a pan over a low heat and simmer with the lemon peel, salt and the vanilla pod with seeds scraped in. It takes about 20–25 minutes for the rice to be completely soft.

Put 2 tablespoons of rice to one side. Add the sugar to the rest of the rice in the pan and blend with a stick blender or using a food processor while it is still hot. It can take a bit of an effort to get it completely smooth. Add the reserved rice to the purée.

When cool, add the cream and chill in the fridge.

Churn in an ice-cream machine according to the manufacturer's instructions, probably for about 30 minutes. Best eaten as soon as it's scoopable, after about 2 hours in the freezer, but this ice cream will keep for a week. Remove from the freezer well ahead of serving to soften once frozen solid.

Serve *affogato* – literally 'drowned' – with grappa, if you like that sort of thing.

RICOTTA ICE CREAM
GELATO ALLA RICOTTA

Super-easy, super-creamy. With figs, hazelnuts and chocolate, I've thrown all the good stuff at this.

FOR 6

100g dried figs

juice of 1 lemon

140g caster sugar

500g ricotta

6 egg yolks

300g double cream

200ml whole milk

70g roasted hazelnuts, chopped into small pieces

80g dark chocolate, chopped into small pieces

Take the tips off the figs and cut into pieces. Put the lemon juice in a pan with 10g of the sugar and the figs. Bring to the boil then turn off the heat and leave to soften.

Pass the ricotta through a sieve and then do it again to make it creamy. Whisk the egg yolks with the rest of the sugar until pale then add the cream, milk and ricotta.

Churn in an ice-cream machine according to the manufacturer's instructions. Towards the end, stir through the nuts, chocolate and figs. Best eaten as soon as it's scoopable, after about 3 hours in the freezer, but this ice cream will keep for a week. Remove from the freezer well ahead of serving to soften once frozen solid.

CHESTNUT RUM RAISIN ICE CREAM

GELATO DI CASTAGNE AL RHUM

This classic flavour combination makes a great winter ice cream.

FOR 6

50ml dark rum

75g raisins

500g chestnuts

300ml whole milk

½ cinnamon stick

1 tbsp honey

100g caster sugar

tiny pinch sea salt

3 egg yolks

cocoa powder and crème fraîche, to serve (optional)

Put the rum in a pan and warm slightly before taking off the heat and soaking the raisins in it until cool again.

Preheat the oven to 200°C/fan 180°C/gas 6. Score and roast the chestnuts for 20 minutes, or until soft, then peel them. (It is possible to microwave the chestnuts if you have one.)

Put half of the milk, 150ml water, the cinnamon, chestnuts, honey, roughly half the sugar and the salt in a pan and simmer for 10 minutes. Remove the cinnamon, purée in a food processor and chill.

Whisk the rest of the sugar with the egg yolks until pale, then add the chestnut purée and the remaining milk and combine.

Churn in an ice-cream machine according to the manufacturer's instructions, adding the rum and raisins halfway through. Best eaten as soon as it's scoopable, after about 1–2 hours in the freezer, but this ice cream will keep for a week. Remove from the freezer well ahead of serving to soften once frozen solid.

Dust with cocoa powder and serve with whipped crème fraîche, if you like.

WHOLE WHEAT ICE CREAM
GELATO DI FARRO

The flavours in this ice cream are borrowed from *pastiera*, the famous Italian Easter pie. It is best eaten the day it is made rather than waiting 40 days, so think carefully about what you give up for Lent.

FOR 6

150g whole wheat (spelt would be best), preferably pearled, soaked overnight in cold water

1.5 litres whole milk

3 strips lemon peel

1 cinnamon stick

150g caster sugar

grated zest of ½ orange

250g ricotta

Drain the wheat and put in a pan with 1 litre of the milk. Add the lemon peel and cinnamon stick and bring to a simmer. Once simmering, knock back the heat, taking care not to scorch the milk – it might well take a long time to cook the wheat, around 1½ hours. During this time add the rest of the milk gradually, stirring from time to time.

When cooked, discard the cinnamon and remove 2 tablespoons of the wheat berries and set aside. Add the sugar to the rest of the wheat and purée in a processor until smooth. Stir in the orange zest and leave to cool completely.

When cold, pass the ricotta through a sieve, twice, and mix through the whole wheat. Chill completely in the fridge.

Churn in an ice-cream machine according to the manufacturer's instructions until thick and creamy. Add the whole wheat grains before freezing. Best eaten as soon as it's scoopable, after about 1–2 hours in the freezer, this ice cream will keep for a week. Remove from the freezer well ahead of serving to soften once frozen solid.

RING BISCUITS
TARALLI DOLCI

Headway is a charity set up for those who have sustained brain injuries and, for a while, I volunteered there. I made these biscuits for the Headway East London pop-up shop. They are not overly sweet and are as happy with a glass of wine as a coffee.

MAKES ABOUT 60

150g semola flour
1 tsp baking powder
1 heaped tsp fennel seeds
½ tsp ground cinnamon
pinch sea salt
30g caster sugar
40ml whole milk
40ml extra virgin olive oil
granulated brown sugar for dipping

Mix the flour, baking powder and spices together in a bowl with the salt and caster sugar. Then add the milk and olive oil. Continue to mix until you have a soft dough. Wrap in cling film and leave to relax for 15 minutes.

Preheat the oven to 190°C/fan 170°C/gas 5 and line a baking tray with baking paper.

Have ready a saucer of the granulated sugar. Roll a walnut-sized piece of dough between the palms of your hands or on the worktop to make a sausage then join the ends together to form a ring. Dip each ring as it is formed into the sugar to coat on one side. Then place on the baking paper sugar side up.

Bake the biscuits for 15 minutes until golden. Allow to cool before eating.

BISCUIT CAKE

FETTE BISCOTTATE

In the bakery in Bisaccia, they still sell 'biscuit' cake. As a lad, they were presented to me by my grandmother with a bowl of steaming milk containing a nip of coffee. This recipe is a sort of version of the biscuit cakes I remember from my childhood. They are twice-baked like biscotti. Also, not overly sweet, these are great with homemade ice cream.

MAKES 24

100g salted butter, plus extra for greasing

50g honey

120g stoneground wholemeal flour, plus extra for dusting

1 tsp baking powder

2 eggs

15g golden caster sugar

1 tsp anise liqueur, whisky or grappa

Preheat the oven to 180°C/fan 160°C/gas 4 and butter and flour a loaf tin.

Melt the butter in a pan and allow it to brown slightly. This will only take a few minutes. Once the butter has changed colour, add the honey and take off the heat.

Mix the flour with the baking powder. In a separate bowl, vigorously whisk the eggs and sugar until very foamy. Then, still whisking, add the alcohol and butter and honey mixture. Fold through the flour to make an unappetising-looking batter.

Pour into the tin and bake for 30 minutes until springy when lightly pressed. Remove from the tin and leave to rest on a rack for 5 minutes before transferring to a baking tray – this is so that it doesn't crumble as you cut it. Slice the cake thinly, using the other hand to carefully hold the cake together. The slices are hardier once re-baked.

Turn the oven down to 170°C/fan 150°C/gas 3. Return the cake slices to the oven and bake for 9 minutes, turning them over halfway through.

GRAPPA SUGAR CUBES

ZUCCHERINI GRAPPA E MENTA

These are used as a digestive. I'm doubtful about the efficacy but, who knows! They do taste nicely medicinal. The idea comes via a Sardinian colleague whose brother makes them. Stir into espresso if you need a kick-start, or have as they are. Either way, only have one – they are lethal.

MAKES 30 CUBES

100g sugar cubes
mint leaves
cloves
100ml grappa

Using a spoon, layer sugar cubes interspersed with unblemished mint leaves and a clove here and there in a sterilised glass jar (see page 94). Then top up with the grappa. Leave them at the back of the cupboard in the dark for at least a month. They will keep well for a year.

WALNUT KISSES

BACI DI NOCI

I once bought a lovely box of exquisite *Baci di Cherasco*: pedigree Piedmontese hazelnut chocolates. It inspired this much more confused but totally delectable confection. I have used other things in these before: coffee beans, seeds, spices, etc. But this version remains my favourite. The trick is to be judicious with the cinnamon and fennel seeds so that they don't take over.

MAKES ABOUT 15

15g butter

25g brown sugar

pinch sea salt

pinch ground cinnamon

pinch fennel seeds

100g shelled fresh walnuts or cobnuts

150g dark chocolate

Have a piece of baking paper stretched out on a board before you begin.

In a pan, melt the butter over a good heat. Add the sugar and salt and when they have melted, sprinkle in the cinnamon, add the fennel seeds and then the nuts.

Allow to caramelise for 2 minutes, stirring with a wooden spoon before scooping onto the baking paper. Allow to cool completely.

Bring a pan of water to the boil. Roughly break two-thirds of the chocolate into a metal bowl that fits into the pan. Place over the water but not touching, and turn off the heat. Leave it alone to allow to melt completely without stirring.

Once melted, remove from the pan, add the rest of the chocolate and wait for that to melt as well. It will be a good deal thicker than when melted all together over water and hopefully won't have lost its temper.

Stretch out a new piece of baking paper over the cooled sugared nuts.

Crunch the nuts inside the paper (bash them with a rolling pin if you like) and dump them into the chocolate and fold through gently.

Teaspoon this mix back onto the baking paper using a spatula to help. When you've done the lot, leave somewhere cold and allow to cool for 30 minutes. If kept sealed and stored somewhere cool they should last a couple of weeks.

CHOCOLATE AMARETTI
AMARETTI AL CIOCCOLATO

Due to their simple nature, these are best eaten as soon as they are cool enough, while still soft. They are so quick to make that if you start now they can easily be gone in under an hour. This is consequently a small batch.

MAKES ABOUT 10

100g blanched almonds

50g golden caster sugar

tiny pinch sea salt

50g dark chocolate, broken into pieces, plus extra to decorate

1 egg white

a couple of scrapes of lemon zest

Preheat the oven to 190°C/fan 170°C/gas 5 and line a baking tray with baking paper.

Put the almonds in a food processor along with half of the sugar and the salt and blitz until very fine – a couple of minutes. Add the chocolate to the mix and continue to buzz until it is fine too.

Whisk the egg white into peaks with an electric beater or by hand. Add the remaining sugar and continue whisking to make a shiny meringue. Grate in the lemon zest and then fold through the almond-chocolate mixture.

Shape tablespoon-sized pieces of dough into rough balls with your fingers, or using a couple of spoons if the mixture is sticky, and line up on the baking tray. Break off an extra shard of chocolate for each one and place in the middle, sitting proud on top.

Bake for 10 minutes. They will look too soft but aren't.

WALNUT, ALMOND AND SOUR CHERRY BISCUITS

BISCOTTI DI NOCI, MANDORLE E AMARENE

These are crunchy on the outside and soft within.

MAKES ABOUT 30

150g walnuts

1 egg white

150g caster sugar

150g blanched almonds

FOR THE ICING

75g icing sugar

50g sour cherries in syrup, drained and sliced with syrup retained

zest of 1 unwaxed lemon

sea salt

Soak the walnuts in fresh water for half an hour.

Whisk the egg white with half of the sugar until stiff, either by hand or with an electric beater.

Grind the almonds to a fine flour in a food processor. Add the rest of the sugar and the drained walnuts and process to a paste. It may take a few goes. Stop and scrape the sides of the bowl several times to help things along. Add the egg white and pulse together.

Scoop the paste onto a sheet of cling film. Roll up and refrigerate for an hour.

Preheat the oven to 190°C/fan 170°C/gas 5 and line a baking tray with baking paper.

Unwrap the dough but keep it lying on the cling film as it is excessively soft. Using a wet butter knife cut off small shapes of dough and, using your little finger, transfer them to the baking tray.

Bake for 8 minutes until just golden on the tips and hardened on the outside. Leave to cool.

In a bowk, mix the icing sugar with a tiny pinch of salt and stir in 2 tablespoons of the cherry syrup and another of water to make a thick paste. Add to this the cherries and use to decorate the biscuits.

Grate over the lemon zest.

CHICKPEA BISCUITS
BISCOTTI DI CECI

I had been feeling nostalgic about the sweet(ish) ravioli-shaped biscuits stuffed with chickpeas and cacao that Nonna used to make at Christmas. Memory plays tricks: I never really liked them when I was small, and when I was offered one recently, I realised that I still don't. These are another matter; still a little eccentric but not quite as edgy. The basis of the recipe comes from a homespun packet of chickpea flour I had. The smell of it toasting in the pan reminds me of something else – just how good dry-roasted chickpeas are as a snack.

MAKES ABOUT 40

275g chickpea flour

130g golden caster sugar

130g almonds

½ tsp baking powder

zest of 1 unwaxed lemon

½ tsp ground ginger

2cm fresh ginger, grated (about 50g)

100ml extra virgin olive oil

2 eggs

melted dark chocolate, to serve (optional)

Preheat the oven to 180°C/fan 160°C/gas 4 and line two large baking trays with baking paper.

Carefully toast the chickpea flour in a large frying pan over the lowest possible heat. It is easy to burn, so stir continuously with a wooden spoon, being sure to scrape the flour from the bottom and edges of the pan. Do this for about 10–15 minutes until the flour has changed colour.

Blitz the sugar with the almonds in a food processor until smooth. Sift the toasted flour into a large bowl with the baking powder and stir in the sugar and almonds, the lemon zest and gingers. Whisk the oil and eggs together before pouring into the flour and incorporating into a dry dough.

On a clean work surface, roll out to a thickness of about 1cm and unstick from the worktop using a palette knife before cutting into rough squares of approximately 4cm.

Transfer the squares to the baking trays and bake for 15–20 minutes, depending on how crunchy you like your biscuits.

When cool dip into or top with just-melted dark chocolate, if you fancy.

SALTY-SWEET 'BROAD BEANS'

FAVE DOLCI

Also known as *Fave dei Morti* (Day of the Dead beans), these are usually made with almonds. Here, I've added pistachios. If you prefer your biscuits without salt, use plain, shelled pistachios for a more vivid colour; but salted are easy to find, and I enjoy the salty-sweet flavour.

MAKES 20

70g shelled salted pistachios

30g almonds

150g caster sugar

50g plain flour

30g butter

1 egg

Blitz the nuts and sugar together in a food processor until completely fine, then add the flour. Pulse. Add the butter. Pulse. Then add the egg and pulse again. Once you have a dough, wrap in cling film and refrigerate.

Preheat the oven to 180°C/fan 160°C/gas 4 and line a baking tray with baking paper. Roll the dough out into small balls the size of broad beans and place on the baking tray. Chill for 15 minutes in the fridge before baking for 10 minutes. Store in an airtight container once cool.

NOUGAT
TORRONE

It is not possible to make this without a proper thermometer and keep your kids out of the kitchen as the hot sugar is dangerous and the recipe needs some concentration. Having said that, it is not complicated and takes just 45 minutes of your life. I have made this and checked the finished product within the time of *The Andrew Marr Show* on a Sunday morning – bliss. Read the recipe through a few times before you attempt it. Once the train is set in motion you have to be methodical and do everything in the right order.

MAKES 6 BARS

3 sheets edible rice paper
50g dates, chopped into pieces
80g candied lemon or lime peel
50g pine nuts
70g toasted hazelnuts
25g pumpkin seeds
120g caster sugar
120g honey
120g liquid glucose
25g egg whites
zest of ½ orange
tiny pinch sea salt
100g unsalted butter, diced

Line a 25cm loaf or other tin with two of the sheets of rice paper. Cut to fit but let it overlap so there are absolutely no gaps.

Preheat the oven to 120°C/fan 100°C/gas ½. Spread the dates, candied peel, nuts and seeds over a baking tray and put in the oven to warm through – you can turn off the oven once they are in.

Weigh half the sugar, honey and glucose into one heavy-based pan and the other half of them into another heavy-based pan. Add 10ml water to each. Bring both slowly to the boil.

In the meantime, whisk the egg whites to soft peaks in a stand mixer. Use a thermometer to check the temperature of the syrups and when one reaches 126°C, pour slowly and carefully into the whites with the mixer still going. Then turn the mixer to slow while the second pot reaches 157°C. When it does, turn the mixer back to high and pour in the syrup. Be careful that it doesn't touch you or hit the sides of the bowl as it will stick like anything. Turn back to slow and gradually mix in the zest, salt and butter bit by bit. Take a whole minute to do this slowly, then leave the mixer running for 4 minutes.

Feel how hot the bowl is by placing your hands on the outside. If you can work with it, turn off the mixer and remove the bowl. Mix through the warmed nuts, seeds and fruit with a wooden spoon and pour into the prepared tin.

Cover with another sheet of rice paper, pressing down well. Once cool enough, refrigerate for several hours until cold. Cut with a sharp knife into squares. This is best stored in the fridge, or at least somewhere cool.

GRAPE CROSTATA
CROSTATA DI UVA

Crostata is the dessert that will follow you around Italy, so there had to be one here too. It is ubiquitous in bakeries and cafés, its crisscrosses of pastry concealing sweet jam of every known colour. This is filled with grapes rather than jam and has nuts in the crust.

FOR 10

FOR THE PASTRY

100g walnuts

250g organic '00' flour

120g golden caster sugar

pinch sea salt (or use salted butter)

1 tbsp baking powder

zest of 1 lemon or orange

120g unsalted butter

3 egg yolks

FOR THE FILLING

500g wine grapes, halved

1 tbsp caster sugar

150ml double cream

100g walnuts

First make the pastry. Blitz the walnuts in a food processor. Mix these in a big bowl with the flour, sugar, salt, baking powder and zest. Melt the butter in a small pan over a medium heat without scorching. Make a well in the middle of your walnut-flour mix and tip in the melted butter and egg yolks. Mix with a fork or spoon and eventually your hands to make a dough. Wrap in cling film and refrigerate for at least 45 minutes.

This dough is too crumbly to roll. Instead take bits and press it into a 20cm tart shell, piece by piece. I like to leave it pretentiously ragged around the edges. Use up about three-quarters of the pastry doing this; it can be quite thick. Then put it in the freezer to firm for 15 minutes while you make the filling.

Preheat the oven to 180°C/fan 160°C/gas 4.

Throw the grapes into a hot pan, allowing them to heat and almost scorch a bit. It should be hot enough that they squeak. Once you've pushed them around, add the sugar and then the cream. Move around the pan and allow to brown and rapidly reduce but not burn. Turn off after 3 minutes and add the walnuts.

Remove the pastry shell from the freezer and line with baking paper topped with dried beans or ceramic weights and blind bake for 10 minutes.

Pour the filling into the tart shell but be careful not to spread it out as the hot pastry will be fragile. Squidge and crumble the rest of the dough into rough pieces and scatter over, leaving gaps here and there.

Return to the oven and bake at 170°C/fan 150°C/gas 3 for 30 minutes before turning the oven down to 150°C/fan 130°C/gas 2 and baking for a further 15 minutes. The top should have a deep colour and the fruit will have condensed.

This is best served while still warm.

PEACH AND RED WINE CROSTATA

CROSTATA DI PESCHE

I can't decide if I like this or the preceding recipe best. You could make infinite other variations on this theme. The idea here comes from a favourite summer dessert, which is peaches in red wine. As a boy, I watched reverently as the Italian men sat at the ends of the table with knives in hand, cutting peaches straight into their replenished glasses of red wine. It struck me as the most manly of things to do and I longed to join in.

FOR 10

FOR THE PASTRY

100g walnuts

250g organic '00' flour

pinch sea salt (or use salted butter)

1 tbsp baking powder

120g unsalted butter

3 egg yolks

120g golden caster sugar

FOR THE FILLING

500g ripe peaches

2 tbsp brown sugar

200ml red wine

To make the pastry, follow the first two steps of the Grape Crostata recipe (page 288), omitting the lemon or orange zest.

To make the filling, cut the peaches into slices about 2cm across. Throw them into a hot pan with the sugar. Stir for 1 minute before adding the wine. Reduce on a high heat for about 8 minutes, or until you have a loose jammy consistency around the fruit slices.

While the peaches are cooking, remove the pastry tin from the freezer and line with baking paper topped with dried beans or ceramic weights and blind bake for 10 minutes.

Pour the filling into the tart shell but be careful not to spread it out as the hot pastry will be fragile. Squidge and crumble the rest of the dough into rough pieces and scatter over, leaving gaps here and there.

Return to the oven and bake at 170°C/fan 150°C/gas 3 for 30 minutes before turning the oven down to 150°C/fan 130°C/gas 2 and baking for a further 15 minutes. The top should have a deep colour and the fruit will have condensed.

ELUSIVE APPLE CAKE
TORTA DI MELE

There is this apple cake that is almost a generic Italian apple cake, but better. It is made for us every year by the mother of a great wine maker who we visit on a work trip and it's a running joke that we can never recreate it back in London. This is not *that* cake but something similar and uses Vin Santo as a tribute to the place it comes from. I make this in throwaway foil containers because that's what they do. When I don't have them, I line a baking tray with baking paper.

FOR 8

120g butter, plus extra for greasing

750g crisp apples

4 eggs, separated

125g golden caster sugar

175ml Vin Santo

150g plain flour

pinch baking powder

icing sugar for dusting

tiny pinch of salt

Preheat the oven to 200°C/fan 180°C/gas 6 and butter a 25cm cake tin.

Melt the butter in a pan over a high heat. Allow it to darken but not burn. Twist the pan so you can see how the colour is changing. I find this fun. Let it arrive at a nutty brown colour. You can even take it a little further than this if you like. Allow to cool but not solidify.

Wash the apples but don't bother to peel them. Quarter them and cut out the cores then slice about 5mm thin.

Whisk the egg yolks with half the sugar until pale. Pour in the melted butter, leaving most of the separated darker pieces at the bottom of the pan. Add the wine. Sift over the flour with the baking powder and salt and gently stir together.

Whisk the egg whites by hand or with an electric beater and, when they make soft peaks, add the remaining sugar in a steady stream, continuing to whisk to make a glossy meringue. Fold a third of the whites into the batter before gently folding in the rest, adding the apple slices towards the end.

Tip the batter into the prepared tin and bake for about 30 minutes, or until golden and springy to touch.

This is a cake best eaten quickly. Dust with icing sugar before you do so.

ITALIAN TRIFLE

ZUPPA INGLESE

I have to add an Italian trifle. It's the perfect Anglo-Italian dessert, with all the goodness of a trifle and none of the bad bits (jelly), plus ricotta. Use whatever soft fruit is in season.

FOR 6

FOR THE CREMA

500ml whole milk

1 vanilla pod, split

100g caster sugar

3 egg yolks

3 tbsp plain flour

FOR THE BERRIES

300ml red wine

75g caster sugar

500g blackberries or other soft fruit

10 mint leaves

FOR THE SPONGE FINGERS

2 eggs, separated

60g caster sugar

50g rye flour

pinch sea salt

FOR THE RICOTTA

500g ricotta

2 egg whites

50g caster sugar

FOR TOPPING

20g Dark Chocolate and Nuts

To make the crema, put the milk in a medium pan over a medium heat and scrape in the seeds from the vanilla pod. When it gets hot, turn the heat down slightly – don't allow it to boil. Whisk together the sugar and egg yolks until pale, then stir in the flour. Whisk a ladleful of the hot milk into the egg mixture to loosen it before whisking it into the rest of the milk, now over a medium-low heat. Cook the custard for 5 minutes, stirring continuously, until thick. Pour into a bowl and continue to stir while it cools. Chill in the fridge.

Next tackle the berries. In a wide pan bring the wine to the boil with the sugar and reduce it over a high heat by two-thirds, then add the fruit. Stir, cooking for a few minutes only, then take off the heat and add the mint leaves.

Preheat the oven to 170°C/fan 150°C/gas 3 and line a baking tray with baking paper. Whisk together the egg yolks and sugar until pale. Mix in the flour. Whisk the egg whites to stiff peaks with the salt. Stir a third of the whites into the yolks before more carefully folding through the remainder. Either pipe or spoon the mix onto the prepared tray to make 10–15 fingers. Bake for 20 minutes. Remove from the paper at once and allow to cool on a rack.

Pass the ricotta through a sieve to make it creamier. Whisk the egg whites to soft peaks before adding the sugar and continuing to whisk until shiny. Fold through the ricotta.

To assemble, arrange a first layer of sponge fingers in the bottom of a serving bowl, pour over some of the juice and a few berries then add a layer of crema, followed by ricotta, then another of sponge fingers, fruit and then crema and finally ricotta.

Chill well before serving and top with grated chocolate and nuts.

INDEX

ABOUT THE AUTHOR

Joseph Trivelli lives in Hammersmith, London with his wife and two children. He is joint head chef at The River Café, where he has worked since 2001. Raised in Kent by his English mother and Italian father, he describes himself as half scone-half pizza. He began his cooking career on the coast in Whitstable in the late 1990s and worked briefly in Australia before landing in London. Sometimes he writes in the *Observer* as understudy to Nigel Slater. He most enjoys cooking at home for his family.

ACKNOWLEDGEMENTS

I would like to thank my parents, Hazel and Antonio for all their love and hard work. Thank you, Mum for the brilliant, responsive paintings and stuffed mushrooms. Dad: for language support and keeping alive family food traditions whilst actually growing new ones. None of your hard work and effort goes unnoticed. Also to my brother, Giacomo and the rest of my family, new and old, especially recipe testers.

To Orion publishers, thank you: Amanda Harris – we got there, albeit some years later; editor, Emily Barrett – for your precision and dedication to the project; and Helen Ewing – for brilliant organisation and overseeing. Matt Russell, your excellent photo-making seems so effortless and working with you is as relaxed as your company. Miranda Harvey, I am really so very grateful for your excellent design and learned experience. Thank you for teaching me how to look properly. Emily Sweet, this was your suggestion, and such a good one. Thank you for making it real. Also Pete Begg, your kind words were as great a help as your incredible cooking. Thank you also Allan Jenkins for giving me a first writing chance. And to my dear old cooking friends Blanche Vaughan, Claire Ptak, Stevie Parle and Tommi Miers.

In Bisaccia, I would like to thank Agostino Pelullo, Peppino Pelullo and Donato Solazzo. For cooking assistance back in London, Georgia Levy, Eliza Dolby, Elliot Bloomfield and Jenna Leiter.

Ruth Rogers, your vision, mentoring, fine taste and sense of fairness is an inspiration for me, as for so many others. Sian Wyn Owen, thank you for your friendship, best man speech and general support. To Charles Pullan, Vashti Armit and all my good friends and colleagues at the River Café. Rose Gray, so much missed, is in everything we do.

Finally, this book is for two people:

My grandmother, Antonietta Pignatiello, who died in March this year after a long, hard but ultimately happy and successful life. Without her as a reference I wouldn't have started cooking, but I owe her much besides my profession. I will never forget the meals that she cooked us full of love and attention. *Impara l'arte e mettila da parte* – learn the craft and keep it safe: if only she knew.

Matilda, my best friend turned in-house editor. A more patient, supportive better forever there cannot be. Look at what getting carried away about Sunday night supper can lead to, my love.

First published in Great Britain in 2018
by Seven Dials
An imprint of Orion Publishing Group Ltd
Carmelite House, 50 Victoria Embankment,
London, EC4Y 0DZ
An Hachette UK Company

10 9 8 7 6 5 4 3 2 1

A CIP catalogue record for this book is available from the British Library.

Hardback ISBN: 9781409174417

Publisher: Amanda Harris
Editor: Emily Barrett
Production controller: Katie Horrocks
Photography: Matt Russell
Design: Miranda Harvey
Props: Lydia Brun
Food styling: Joe Trivelli
Painted illustrations credit: Hazel Trivelli
Fork illustrations: Shutterstock
Pasta illustrations on p23: Nici Holland

Printed and bound in Italy

The Orion Publishing Group's policy is to use papers that are natural, renewable and recyclable products and made of wood from well-managed, FSC®-certified forests and other controlled sources in sustainable forests.
www.orionbooks.co.uk